ESSENTIAL SQA EXAM PRACTICE

OVER 100

QUESTIONS & PAPERS

HIGHER PHYSICS Practice Questions & Exam Papers

Practise **60+ questions** covering every question type and topic

Complete **2 practice papers** that mirror the real SQA exams

Paul Chambers
Mark Ramsay

HODDER GIBSON
AN HACHETTE UK COMPANY

The Publishers would like to thank the following for permission to reproduce copyright material.

Photo credits

page 49 © AA World Travel Library/Alamy Stock Photo

Acknowledgements

Every effort has been made to trace all copyright holders, but if any have been inadvertently overlooked, the Publishers will be pleased to make the necessary arrangements at the first opportunity.

Although every effort has been made to ensure that website addresses are correct at time of going to press, Hodder Gibson cannot be held responsible for the content of any website mentioned in this book. It is sometimes possible to find a relocated web page by typing in the address of the home page for a website in the URL window of your browser.

Hachette UK's policy is to use papers that are natural, renewable and recyclable products and made from wood grown in well-managed forests and other controlled sources. The logging and manufacturing processes are expected to conform to the environmental regulations of the country of origin.

Orders: please contact Bookpoint Ltd, 130 Park Drive, Milton Park, Abingdon, Oxon OX14 4SE. Telephone: (44) 01235 827827. Fax: (44) 01235 400401. Email education@bookpoint.co.uk. Lines are open from 9 a.m. to 5 p.m., Monday to Friday, with a 24-hour message answering service. Visit our website at www.hoddereducation.co.uk. If you have queries or questions that aren't about an order you can contact us at hoddergibson@hodder.co.uk.

First published in 2019 by

Hodder Gibson, an imprint of Hodder Education

An Hachette UK Company

211 St Vincent Street

Glasgow G2 5QY

Impression number	5	4	3	2	1
Year	2023	2022	2021	2020	2019

Illustrations by Aptara Inc.

Typeset in India by Aptara Inc.

Printed and bound by CPI Group (UK) Ltd, Croydon CR0 4YY

A catalogue record for this title is available from the British Library.

ISBN: 978 1 5104 7183 2

SCOTLAND EXCEL

We are an approved supplier on the Scotland Excel framework.

Schools can find us on their procurement system as:

Hodder & Stoughton Limited t/a Hodder Gibson.

CONTENTS

Introduction   iv

Key Area index grids   vii

Relationships sheet   xi

Data sheet   xiii

Practice Questions   1
    Question type: Multiple-choice   1
    Question type: Extended   12

Answers to Practice Questions   33

Practice Exams   45
    Practice Exam A   45
    Practice Exam B   65

Answers to Practice Exams   84
    Answers to Practice Exam A   84
    Answers to Practice Exam B   95

Higher Physics

The assessment materials included in this book are designed to provide practice and to support revision for the Higher Physics course assessment question paper (the examination), which is worth 80% of the final grade for this course.

The materials are provided:

Practice Questions

Practice Exams: Practice Exam A and Practice Exam B

Practice Questions

In the Practice Questions section of this book you will find lots of exam-style practice questions. These consist of multiple-choice questions and extended questions. Each of these are divided into the three main areas of knowledge and understanding of the course content, to aid you with your revision: Our dynamic Universe, Particle and waves, and Electricity.

Linking questions to course specification

Each of the three main areas of knowledge and understanding are further split into 'Key Areas'. These have been numbered in the margin, so that as you work through the book you can identify which Key Areas you are scoring well in and which Key Areas you need to focus your revision on further.

Our dynamic Universe (ODU)

▶ ODU1 Motion – equations and graphs

▶ ODU2 Forces, energy and power

▶ ODU3 Collisions, explosions and impulse

▶ ODU4 Gravitation

▶ ODU5 Special relativity

▶ ODU6 The expanding Universe

Particles and waves (PW)

▶ PW1 Forces on charged particles

▶ PW2 The Standard Model

▶ PW3 Nuclear reactions

▶ PW4 Inverse square law

▶ PW5 Wave–particle duality

▶ PW6 Interference

▶ PW7 Spectra

▶ PW8 Refraction of light

Electricity (E)

▶ E1 Monitoring and measuring AC

▶ E2 Current, potential difference, power and resistance

▶ E3 Electrical sources and internal resistance

▶ E4 Capacitors

▶ E5 Semiconductors and p–n junctions

Question types

In general, there are only a few types of question which are used in the examination paper. The command term used indicates the kind of response you are required to give. Commonly used command terms include: calculate, show that ..., determine, sketch, draw, state (what is meant by), state (the value of), explain (what happens to ...) and 'using your knowledge'. You will find advice on how to answer questions with each of these command terms on pages 12–14.

Practice Papers

Practice Exam A and Practice Exam B

The book contains two full practice exams worth 155 marks (unscaled). These papers are designed to be similar to the actual exams you will sit. They will generally follow the same order, have the same structure and will contain questions of the type that you will encounter in your examination.

Paper 1 – Objective test. This contains 25 multiple-choice items worth 1 mark each and totalling 25 marks altogether.

Paper 2 – This contains restricted- and extended-response questions totalling 130 marks. In the exam this is scaled to 95.

In the SQA examination papers:

▶ approximately 40% of the marks will be awarded for questions related to Our dynamic Universe

▶ approximately 40% of the marks will be awarded for questions related to Particles and waves

▶ approximately 20% of the marks will be awarded for questions related to Electricity

▶ a data booklet or sheet containing relevant data and relationships will be provided.

Grading

To achieve an award of an A grade you generally must achieve a score of more than 70% in your course assessment.

This book does not take into account your assignment, therefore to achieve an 'equivalent' A grade you would need to have a combined score of 84/120. To achieve an 'equivalent' C grade you would need a combined score of 60/120.

If you are looking at this strategically, 5 marks in the multiple-choice paper are worth 5 marks, and 5 marks in the extended questions paper, when scaled, are worth 4 marks.

Timing

The examination assessment will be split into two sittings: **45 minutes** for the multiple-choice paper and **2 hours and 15 minutes** for the written paper. If you are attempting a full practice exam in this book, limit yourself to **3 hours** to complete it.

Practice Exam Key Area index

The Practice Exam Key Area index on pages vii–x shows the pattern of coverage of the Key Areas and the skills across the Practice Exams. After having worked on questions from Key Areas across an area of study, you might want to use the boxes to assess your progress. We suggest marking like this [–] if you are having difficulty (less than half marks), like this [+] if you are more comfortable (more than half marks), and this [*] if you are confident you have learned and understood an entire area of study (nearly full marks). Alternatively, you could use a 'traffic light' system using colours – red for 'not understood', orange for 'more work needed' and green for 'fully understood'. **If you continue to struggle with a set of Key Area questions, you should see your teacher for extra help.**

Using the questions and practice exams

We recommend working between attempting questions or practice exams and studying the answers (see below).

Where any difficulty is encountered, it's worth trying to consolidate your knowledge and skills. Use the information in the 'student margin' to identify the type of question you find trickiest. Be aware that challenge with A-type questions is to be expected.

You will need a **pen**, a **sharp pencil**, a **clear plastic ruler** and a **calculator** for the best results. A couple of different **coloured highlighters** could also be handy.

Answers

The answers for the Practice Questions are provided on pages 33–44, and the answers for the Practice Exams on pages 84–106. They give National Standard answers but, occasionally, there may be other acceptable answers.

The answers to the Practice Exams also have a *Commentary with hints and tips* provided alongside each. These focus on the correct physics, as well as hints, advice on wording of answers and notes of commonly made errors.

General points on awarding of marks

Positive marking

Marks will be awarded for correct physics; marks will not be lost for errors or omissions. Once you have gained a mark in a question it cannot be overturned or removed by a later, incorrect answer. This does not mean that you will gain marks for wrong or missing physics. The unit, for example, will form part of the answer.

Unless working is specifically asked for, a correct final answer will receive full marks. If a question asks you to show how you achieved the value, the marks are for the working.

In 'show' questions you must always start with a relationship. If you do not include the correct relationship in a 'show' question you cannot obtain the full marks.

Marks will be awarded regardless of spelling, as long as the meaning is unambiguous. The spelling of similar words such as fusion/fission needs to be clear and unambiguous.

Rounding: the significant figure(s) of the final answer can have one figure less or two figures more than the expected answer.

Standard numerical questions

There are techniques you can follow in the setting out of your answer which will minimise the possibility of simplistic errors. When setting out your working, allow the marker to give marks for correct physics.

Arithmetical errors will be penalised. An incorrect formula can be interpreted as wrong physics and in these cases the question will be deemed as 'wrong' and the marker will stop marking.

Read the question carefully and gather the data from the question on one side of the page. Ensure you are using standard symbols as this will reduce the possibility of selecting an incorrect relationship.

Revision

There are 19 Key Areas from all three topics of the course content, so covering two each week would require about a 10-week revision programme.

We wish you the very best of luck!

KEY AREA INDEX GRIDS

Practice Exam A

	Paper 1	Paper 2				Check
Key area	Multiple choice	Calculate/ show that	Determine/ sketch/ draw	State/ explain/ describe	Use your knowledge	
Our dynamic Universe ODU1 Motion – equations and graphs	1, 2, 3	1ai, 1b, 1c, 2a	1aii			15
ODU2 Forces, energy and power	4, 5	2b, 2c				8
ODU3 Collisions, explosions and impulse	6	3a, 3c		3b		10
ODU4 Gravitation	7	4a, 4b		4c		10
ODU5 Special relativity		5				3
ODU6 The expanding Universe	8, 9	6a, 6c		6b		9
Particles and waves PW1 Forces on charged particles	14, 15, 16, 17	8bi, 8bii, 8biii	8a		9, 16	20
PW2 The Standard Model	10, 11, 12, 13			7a, 7b		7
PW3 Nuclear reactions	18	10c, 10d		10a, 10b		12
PW4 Inverse square law	21					1
PW5 Wave–particle duality		11c	11d	11a, 11b		9
PW6 Interference	19	12b		12a, 12c		11
PW7 Spectra		14b		14a		5
PW8 Refraction of light	20	13bii	13a	13bi		10

		Paper 1	Paper 2				Check
	Key area	Multiple choice	Calculate/ show that	Determine/ sketch/ draw	State/ explain/ describe	Use your knowledge	
Electricity	E1 Monitoring and measuring AC	22	15a, 15b				☐ 9
	E2 Current, potential difference, power and resistance						☐ 0
	E3 Electrical sources and internal resistance			17b, 17c	17a		☐ 7
	E4 Capacitors	23	18a, 18b				☐ 7
	E5 Semiconductors and p–n junctions	24, 25					☐ 2
						Total	155

Practice Exam B

Key area	Paper 1	Paper 2				Check
	Multiple choice	Calculate/ show that	Determine/ sketch/ draw	State/ explain/ describe	Use your knowledge	
Our dynamic Universe						
ODU1 Motion – equations and graphs	1, 4, 5	1a, 1bi, 1bii, 1biii	1biv, 1bv			☐ 19
ODU2 Forces, energy and power	2, 6, 7	2a, 2b, 2c, 3a, 3b, 13		3c		☐ 20
ODU3 Collisions, explosions and impulse	3	4a, 4b, 4c, 4d		4e		☐ 13
ODU4 Gravitation	8, 9					☐ 2
ODU5 Special relativity	10	5a, 5b				☐ 6
ODU6 The expanding Universe	11, 14	6a, 6b, 6c, 7a		7b, 7c		☐ 19
Particles and waves						
PW1 Forces on charged particles	12, 13				8, 14	☐ 8
PW2 The Standard Model	15, 16			9a, 9b, 9c		☐ 8
PW3 Nuclear reactions	25		10a	10b		☐ 9
PW4 Inverse square law	17	11b	11a	11c		☐ 7
PW5 Wave–particle duality		12a, 12b		12c		☐ 9
PW6 Interference	18					☐ 1
PW7 Spectra						☐ 0
PW8 Refraction of light	19	15a, 15b				☐ 7

	Paper 1	Paper 2				Check
Key area	Multiple choice	Calculate/ show that	Determine/ sketch/ draw	State/ explain/ describe	Use your knowledge	
E1 Monitoring and measuring AC						☐ 0
E2 Current, potential difference, power and resistance	21, 22					☐ 3
E3 Electrical sources and internal resistance		16ai, 16aii, 17a		16b		☐ 10
E4 Capacitors	20, 23	17b, 17di, 17dii	17c			☐ 13
E5 Semiconductors and p–n junctions	24					☐ 1
					Total	155

(Row label spanning E1–E5: Electricity)

RELATIONSHIPS SHEET

You will be provided with a Relationships sheet like this in your final exam. Refer to this as required for each Practice Exam.

$d = \bar{v}t$

$s = \bar{v}t$

$v = u + at$

$s = ut + \frac{1}{2}at^2$

$v^2 = u^2 + 2as$

$s = \frac{1}{2}(u+v)t$

$W = mg$

$F = ma$

$E_w = Fd$

$E_p = mgh$

$E_k = \frac{1}{2}mv^2$

$P = \dfrac{E}{t}$

$p = mv$

$Ft = mv - mu$

$F = G\dfrac{m_1 m_2}{r^2}$

$t' = \dfrac{t}{\sqrt{1 - \left(\dfrac{v}{c}\right)^2}}$

$l' = l\sqrt{1 - \left(\dfrac{v}{c}\right)^2}$

$z = \dfrac{\lambda_{observed} - \lambda_{rest}}{\lambda_{rest}}$

$z = \dfrac{v}{c}$

$v = H_0 d$

$f_o = f_s\left(\dfrac{v}{v \pm v_s}\right)$

$W = QV$

$E = mc^2$

$E = hf$

$E_k - E_1 = hf$

$T = \dfrac{1}{f}$

$v = f\lambda$

$d\sin\theta = m\lambda$

$n = \dfrac{\sin\theta_1}{\sin\theta_2}$

$\dfrac{\sin\theta_1}{\sin\theta_2} = \dfrac{\lambda_1}{\lambda_2} = \dfrac{v_1}{v_2}$

$\sin\theta_c = \dfrac{1}{n}$

$I = \dfrac{k}{d^2}$

$I = \dfrac{P}{A}$

$V_{peak} = \sqrt{2}\,V_{rms}$

$I_{peak} = \sqrt{2}\,I_{rms}$

$Q = It$

$V = IR$

$P = IV = I^2 R = \dfrac{V^2}{R}$

$R_T = R_1 + R_2 + \ldots.$

$\dfrac{1}{R_T} = \dfrac{1}{R_1} + \dfrac{1}{R_2} + \ldots.$

$E = V + Ir$

$V_1 = \left(\dfrac{R_1}{R_1 + R_2}\right)V_s$

$\dfrac{V_1}{V_2} = \dfrac{R_1}{R_2}$

$C = \dfrac{Q}{V}$

$E = \frac{1}{2}QV = \frac{1}{2}CV^2 = \frac{1}{2}\dfrac{Q^2}{C}$

path difference $= m\lambda$ or $\left(m + \frac{1}{2}\right)\lambda$ where $m = 0, 1, 2\ldots$

$\text{random uncertainty} = \dfrac{\text{max. value} - \text{min. value}}{\text{number of values}}$

Additional relationships

Circle

circumference $= 2\pi r$

area $= \pi r^2$

Sphere

surface area $= 4\pi r^2$

volume $= \frac{4}{3}\pi r^3$

Trigonometry

$\sin\theta = \dfrac{\text{opposite}}{\text{hypotenuse}}$

$\cos\theta = \dfrac{\text{adjacent}}{\text{hypotenuse}}$

$\tan\theta = \dfrac{\text{opposite}}{\text{adjacent}}$

$\sin^2\theta + \cos^2\theta = 1$

DATA SHEET

Common physical quantities

Quantity	Symbol	Value	Quantity	Symbol	Value
Speed of light in vacuum	c	$3.00 \times 10^8 \, \text{m s}^{-1}$	Planck's constant	h	$6.63 \times 10^{-34} \, \text{J s}$
Magnitude of the charge on an electron	e	$1.60 \times 10^{-19} \, \text{C}$	Mass of electron	m_e	$9.11 \times 10^{-31} \, \text{kg}$
Universal constant of gravitation	G	$6.67 \times 10^{-11} \, \text{m}^3 \, \text{kg}^{-1} \, \text{s}^{-2}$	Mass of neutron	m_n	$1.675 \times 10^{-27} \, \text{kg}$
Gravitational acceleration on Earth	g	$9.8 \, \text{m s}^{-2}$	Mass of proton	m_p	$1.673 \times 10^{-27} \, \text{kg}$
Hubble's constant	H_0	$2.3 \times 10^{-18} \, \text{s}^{-1}$	Speed of sound in air	v	$3.4 \times 10^2 \, \text{m s}^{-1}$

Refractive indices

The refractive indices refer to sodium light of wavelength 589 nm and to substances at a temperature of 273 K.

Substance	Refractive index	Substance	Refractive index
Diamond	2.42	Water	1.33
Crown glass	1.50	Air	1.00

Spectral lines

Element	Wavelength (nm)	Colour	Element	Wavelength (nm)	Colour
Hydrogen	656	Red	Cadmium	644	Red
	486	Blue-green		509	Green
	434	Blue-violet		480	Blue
	410	Violet			
	397	Ultraviolet			
	389	Ultraviolet			
Sodium	589	Yellow			

Lasers

Element	Wavelength (nm)	Colour
Carbon dioxide	9550 10590 }	Infrared
Helium-neon	633	Red

Properties of selected materials

Substance	Density (kg m^{-3})	Melting point (K)	Boiling point (K)
Aluminium	2.70×10^3	933	2623
Copper	8.96×10^3	1357	2853
Ice	9.20×10^2	273	....
Sea Water	1.02×10^3	264	377
Water	1.00×10^3	273	373
Air	1.29	....	....
Hydrogen	9.0×10^{-2}	14	20

The gas densities refer to a temperature of 273 K and a pressure of 1.01×10^5 Pa.

Question type: Multiple-choice

≫ HOW TO ANSWER

Do not expect all the multiple-choice questions to be easy. Some are straightforward and some are difficult. Although all multiple-choice questions are worth 1 mark, some require more work than a 1-mark question in an extended questions paper, so do not be concerned if you are performing two or three calculations in order to reach an answer.

In Higher Physics there is one correct answer to each multiple-choice question. There are also four wrong answers designed to distract you (distractors). If you can, work out an answer before looking at the possible answers given in the question.

Top Tip!

A good way to avoid being distracted is to cover the possible answers while you read and think about the question.

Top Tip!

Do not spend too much time on one question. Allocate a maximum of two minutes for any individual question. Do not be concerned if some questions are answered immediately and others require a lot of consideration. This is normal in these types of questions.

If you are not confident about an answer, you can improve your chances by eliminating the answers that you know are definitely wrong. Answers can be eliminated for a number of reasons, such as incorrect unit, a velocity greater than the speed of light or a value for an answer that is out by a large factor (for example, mass of astronaut 300 kg). Occasionally distractors are obvious.

In the exam, if you cannot achieve an answer that is one of the responses, put a line through one of the boxes in the answer grid; any answer has a 1 in 5 chance of being correct.

Where a question is complicated, write down notes and working on the blank pages at the end of the question paper or beside the actual question. Do not use the answer grid for working. Remember to cross out any rough working for these multiple-choice questions when you have finished.

Our dynamic Universe

1 Which of the following could you determine from a speed–time graph?

A   power

B   force

C   distance

D   displacement

E   momentum

Our dynamic Universe 1

2 The graph shows the velocity–time relationship for a ball dropped from a height at time $t = 0$.

Between which points is the ball in contact with the ground?

A   1 and 2

B   3 and 4

C   5 and 6

D   2 and 3, and 4 and 5

E   3 and 4, and 5 and 6

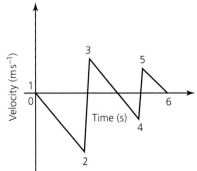

Our dynamic Universe 1

3 A ball has a potential energy of 1·5J when raised. It is dropped and hits the ground at 2ms^{-1}.

Assuming no energy losses, the mass of the ball is

A   0·15kg

B   0·375kg

C   0·75kg

D   1·50kg

E   3·00kg.

Our dynamic Universe 2

4 A block of mass 5·00kg slides down a slope at an angle of 40°. Identify the correct component of weight acting parallel to the slope and acting normal to the slope from the table.

	Parallel	Normal
A	41·1N	37·5N
B	31·5N	41·1N
C	31·5N	37·5N
D	37·5N	31·5N
E	37·5N	41·1N

Our dynamic Universe 2

5 A 4·0kg box slides with a constant velocity down a slope.

The slope makes an angle of 30° with the horizontal.

What is the value of the force of friction acting on the box?

A   0N

B   2·0N

C   19·6N

D   22·6N

E   33·9N

Our dynamic Universe 2

6 The graph shows the speed–time relationship for a parachutist's journey from the aircraft to the ground.

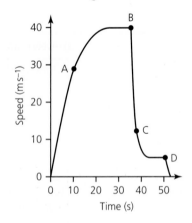

Which statement describes the forces acting on the parachutist between points B and C?

A   Weight force is greater than upthrust.

B   Weight force is less than upthrust.

C   Weight force is equal to upthrust.

D   Weight force is zero.

E   Upthrust is zero.

Our dynamic Universe 2

7 The forces acting on an object are shown in the diagram.

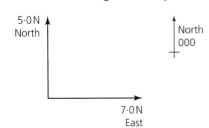

Which of the following is the resultant force vector acting on the object?

A 8·6 N at 036

B 8·6 N at 054

C 12 N at 036

D 12 N at 054

E 5 N at 036

Our dynamic Universe 2

8 A 3·5 kg mass is raised through a height of 2·4 m in 30 seconds using an electric winch.

What is the minimum power output of the electric winch motor?

A 8·4 J

B 8·4 W

C 2·7 J

D 2·7 W

E 105 W

Our dynamic Universe 2

9 A missile explodes into two fragments, X and Y. One piece (X) moves off with a velocity of 48 m s^{-1}; the other (Y) moves off in the opposite direction with a velocity of 24 m s^{-1}.

Which one of the following statements is true?

A X has the same mass as Y.

B X has half the mass of Y.

C X has twice the mass of Y.

D X has three times the mass of Y.

E X has a third the mass of Y.

Our dynamic Universe 3

10 A stationary golf ball of mass 170 g is struck by a golf club. The force–time graph is shown below.

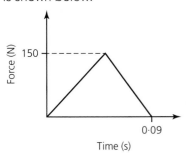

What is the velocity of the ball immediately after impact?

A 0·06 m s^{-1}

B 3·6 m s^{-1}

C 40 m s^{-1}

D 79 m s^{-1}

E 4900 m s^{-1}

Our dynamic Universe 3

11 A mass is projected off a cliff.

Which of the following statements is/are true?

I   The horizontal acceleration is zero.

II   The horizontal velocity is constant.

III   The vertical acceleration is zero.

A   I only

B   II only

C   III only

D   I and II only

E   I and III only

12 A spacecraft moving towards the Earth at $2 \cdot 0 \times 10^8 \, \text{m s}^{-1}$ has a forward-facing laser directed towards the Earth. The speed of the light received is measured by a stationary observer on the Earth's surface.

What is the speed of light measured by the observer?

A $1 \cdot 0 \times 10^8 \, \text{m s}^{-1}$

B $2 \cdot 0 \times 10^8 \, \text{m s}^{-1}$

C $3 \cdot 0 \times 10^8 \, \text{m s}^{-1}$

D $4 \cdot 0 \times 10^8 \, \text{m s}^{-1}$

E $5 \cdot 0 \times 10^8 \, \text{m s}^{-1}$

13 A distant galaxy is moving away from the Earth and the light it emits is analysed to determine the wavelength of its spectral lines. A particular line is measured to have $\lambda = 700 \, \text{nm}$. The same line emitted from a gas sample on Earth has $\lambda = 630 \, \text{nm}$.

The redshift of the distant galaxy is

A $0 \cdot 1$

B $0 \cdot 11$

C $0 \cdot 9$

D $1 \cdot 11$

E $5 \cdot 89$.

14 We can estimate the mass of a galaxy by

A   the peak irradiance wavelength emitted by the stars within it

B   the recession velocity of the galaxy

C   the distance between the Earth and the galaxy

D   the redshift of the light emitted by the stars within it

E   the orbital speed of stars within it.

15 A car is travelling towards a stationary person at $25 \, \text{m s}^{-1}$. It sounds its horn, which operates at $750 \, \text{Hz}$.

What is the frequency heard by the observer?

A $695 \, \text{Hz}$

B $725 \, \text{Hz}$

C $750 \, \text{Hz}$

D $775 \, \text{Hz}$

E $810 \, \text{Hz}$

16 Dark matter has been proposed as an unusual form of non-baryonic matter which is responsible for most of the matter in the Universe.

The main evidence for its existence comes from

A   the temperature of stars in distant galaxies

B   the rate of rotation of galaxies

C   the cosmic microwave background radiation

D   stellar growth and formation

E   particles found very shortly after the Big Bang.

Particles and waves

17 One type of baryon consists of two up quarks and one down quark.

The charge on a down quark is $-\frac{1}{3}$.

The charge on an up quark is $+\frac{2}{3}$.

Which row in the table shows the charge and type for this baryon?

	Charge	Type of baryon
A	+1	neutron
B	0	neutron
C	−1	neutron
D	−1	proton
E	+1	proton

18 Which of the following statements is/are true?

I Quarks are fermions.

II Leptons are fermions.

III Force-mediating particles are bosons.

A I only

B II only

C III only

D I and II only

E I, II and III

19 In an experiment, a student connects a length of copper wire to a 6V supply. They notice that small plotting compasses change direction slightly when the circuit is connected.

This is because

A the current in the copper attracts the North section of the compasses

B the charges in the copper become magnetic and attract the compasses

C the energy in the wire is dissipated as heat and interferes with the surrounding area

D the copper aligns itself with the magnetic field from the compasses

E the magnetic field produced by the charges moving in the copper wire affects the compasses.

20 A student describes an electric field with the following statements.

I A charge in an electric field will experience a balanced force.

II A charge in the field will move downwards.

III When an electric field is applied to a conductor, the free charges in the conductor move.

Which statements is/are correct?

A I and II only

B I, II and III

C I only

D II only

E III only

21 This graph was obtained from an experiment on the photoelectric effect.

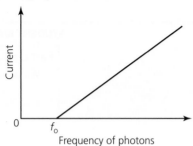

A student makes the following statements:

I   Below the threshold frequency, f_0, no electrons are ejected.

II   More electrons are ejected as the frequency of the photons increases.

II   Frequency, f_0, is the minimum frequency at which a neutron will be ejected.

Which of these statements is/are correct?

A   I only

B   II only

C   III only

D   I and II only

E   I, II and III

22 Electromagnetic radiation of frequency 9.5×10^{14} Hz is incident on a section of metal. The work function of the metal is 5.2×10^{-19} J.

The maximum kinetic energy of a photoelectron released from the surface is

A 1.1×10^{-19} J

B 2.5×10^{-19} J

C 4.3×10^{-19} J

D 5.2×10^{-19} J

E 6.3×10^{-19} J.

23 Monochromatic light of wavelength λ passes through a grating and produces a pattern of bright maxima on a screen. The separation of lines is d and the grating is at a distance L from the screen.

Which changes will produce an increase in the spacing of maxima on the screen?

A   increase L; increase d

B   increase λ; increase d

C   decrease L; decrease λ

D   increase L; decrease λ

E   increase λ; decrease d

24 Two loudspeakers are connected to the same signal generator. During an experiment, the first minimum from the central position is observed at point X, as shown in the diagram.

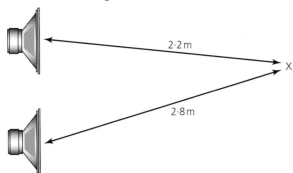

What is the frequency of the sound wave?

A   12 Hz

B   34 Hz

C   283 Hz

D   567 Hz

E   850 Hz

25 In an optics experiment, a ray of light is seen to travel between two transparent materials, as shown.

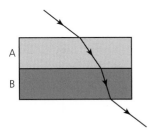

What can be concluded from this diagram?

A   The frequency of the light in material A is greater than the frequency in air.

B   The velocity of light in material B is greater than the velocity in material A.

C   Material B has a greater refractive index than material A.

D   Material A has a greater refractive index than material B.

E   The wavelength of light in material A and material B is the same.

26 Light is shone from a ray box into a block of plastic, as shown in the diagram.

Using the information provided in this diagram, find the refractive index of the plastic.

A   0·87

B   1·06

C   1·15

D   1·51

E   1·63

Particles and waves 8

27 Light from a filament lamp is passed through a glass prism and a spectrum is produced. The white light separates into its constituent frequencies, which we observe as different colours.

How can this be explained?

A   White light is a mixture of these frequencies.

B   Different frequencies travel at different velocities and so take different times to travel through the prism, leading to separation.

C   The white light combines while inside the glass to produce different frequencies upon leaving.

D   Different frequencies have different refractive indices and travel at different angles as a result.

E   The angles of the prism cause different frequencies to refract unequally.

Particles and waves 7

28 A student measures the irradiance of light from a point source at various distances and notes the following results.

Irradiance (W m^{-2})	Distance (m)
45·0	0·05
5·0	0·15
1·8	0·25
0·2	0·75

The irradiance of the light at a distance of 1·1 m from the source is

A   0·15 W m^{-2}

B   0·93 W m^{-2}

C   0·050 W m^{-2}

D   0·093 W m^{-2}

E   0·0093 W m^{-2}.

Particles and waves 4

29 The photon energies for three different radiations are as follows.

Radiation 1: $2{\cdot}78 \times 10^{-19}$ J

Radiation 2: $5{\cdot}24 \times 10^{-19}$ J

Radiation 3: $6{\cdot}35 \times 10^{-19}$ J

Which statement is correct?

A   The wavelength of radiation 1 is longer than that of radiation 2.

B   The wavelength of radiation 3 is longer than that of radiation 2.

C   The frequency of radiation 1 is higher than that of radiation 2.

D   The frequency of radiation 1 is higher than that of radiation 3.

E   The frequency of radiation 2 is higher than that of radiation 3.

> Particles and waves 5

30 Light from the Sun was analysed and its spectrum was observed. Close inspection found many small gaps in the spectrum. They appear as fine, dark lines.

The lines are caused by

A   gases in the outer layers of the Sun absorbing photons

B   the central core of the Sun, which does not emit light across the whole spectrum

C   the dissipation of certain colours as the photons travel the long distance from the Sun to Earth

D   the upper atmosphere of the Earth blocking certain colours

E   the light from the Sun being refracted and diffracted on its journey to Earth.

> Particles and waves 7

Electricity

31 An alternating voltage is displayed on an oscilloscope screen, as shown.

The time-base control is set to 8 ms/div.

The Y-gain control is set to 0·5 mV/div.

> Electricity 1

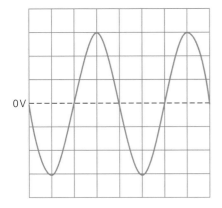

0 V

Which row in the table shows the correct frequency and peak voltage of the output signal?

	Frequency (Hz)	Peak voltage (V)
A	31·25	0·0015
B	31·25	1·5
C	62·5	667
D	125	1·5
E	125	0·0015

32 A circuit is set up as shown.

The r.m.s. voltage across the lamp is 9·0 V. The resistance of the lamp is 3·0 Ω.

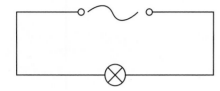

The peak current in the lamp is

  A 0·5 A

  B 2·1 A

  C 3·0 A

  D 4·2 A

  E 2·7 A.

Electricity 1

33 The resistivity of a wire is given by the relationship

$$\rho = \frac{RA}{l}$$

where:

R is the resistance of the wire

A is the cross-sectional area of the wire

l is the length of the wire.

The resistivity of a particular wire is $6·2 \times 10^{-8}\,\Omega\,\text{m}$.

The length of this wire is 65 m.

The wire has a circular cross section of radius 5 mm.

The resistance of the wire is

  A 0·0075 Ω

  B 0·05 Ω

  C 0·062 Ω

  D 0·065 Ω

  E 0·075 Ω.

Electricity 2

34 A student is investigating the following light-sensing circuit. The resistance of the variable resistor is set to 6 kΩ.

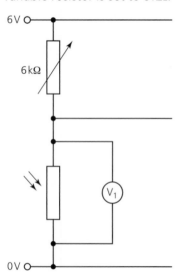

Electricity 2

At a certain light level, the voltage V_1 is measured to be 1·50V.

What is the current in the light-dependent resistor at this light level?

A   0·25 mA

B   0·75 mA

C   1·00 mA

D   2·25 mA

E   3·00 mA

35 A student is given the following information about a capacitor: the energy stored when the capacitor is fully charged and the size of the capacitor.

What relationship could the student use to calculate the charge held by the capacitor?

A $Q = \sqrt{2EC}$

B $Q = \sqrt{EC}$

C $Q = 2EC$

D $Q = \dfrac{\sqrt{EC}}{2}$

E $Q = 2EC^2$

Electricity 4

36 A 46 µF capacitor is connected to a 9V DC supply. The supply is then increased to 15V DC.

The gain in energy is

A $0·21 \times 10^{-3}$ J

B $0·35 \times 10^{-3}$ J

C $1·9 \times 10^{-3}$ J

D $3·3 \times 10^{-3}$ J

E $5·2 \times 10^{-3}$ J.

Electricity 4

37 In a photodiode, which of the following happens when a photon enters an n-type semiconductor?

A   The photon is converted to an electron and aids conduction.

B   The photon is absorbed by an electron.

C   The photon replaces an electron.

D   The energy of the photon enables an electron to move from the valence to the conduction band.

E   The energy of the photon is emitted as light.

Electricity 5

Question type: Extended

❯❯ HOW TO ANSWER

In the Higher Physics exam, Paper 2 contains extended questions worth from 3 to around 16 marks each, totalling 130 marks altogether.

In general, there are only a few types of question which are used. Below are the question types listed by the command term used in the question, with guidance on how to construct a response to each type.

Calculate

Use a relationship from the relationship sheet to calculate a value for the quantity in the question.

▶ Write down the appropriate relationship as written in the Relationship sheet.
▶ Convert any number in the question to standard units (for example, km to m), preferably using scientific notation (for example, km to $\times 10^3$ m).
▶ Substitute the (converted) numbers from the question into the relationship.
▶ Use a calculator to perform the calculation.
▶ Write down the answer
   ● with units
   ● to appropriate precision, i.e. the fewest number of significant figures in the question.

This is usually a 3-mark question, with marks given for the selection of the correct relationship (1), number substitution (1) and correct answer with units (1).

> **Top Tip!**
>
> Full marks will be given for just the correct answer with units but it is always better to show the complete working in order to avoid lost marks for careless errors in the final answer.

Show that

This is similar to 'calculate', but the answer is given in the question. The approach should be the same as the above. However, the second mark is not awarded if the numerical answer and units are not shown.

▶ Write down the appropriate relationship as given in the paper.
▶ Convert any number in the question to standard units (for example, km to m), preferably using scientific notation (for example, km to $\times 10^3$ m).
▶ Substitute the (converted) numbers from the question into the relationship.
▶ Use a calculator to perform the calculation.
▶ Write down the answer
   ● with units
   ● to appropriate precision, i.e. the fewest number of significant figures in the question.

Note that this answer will most likely be used in the subsequent part of a question. The reason for a 'show that' style question is to allow candidates to gain access to the later marks in a question.

If you do not achieve the given answer you can still use the given answer to continue with the question. Using the given answer, not your calculated answer, to continue the question is advised as there may be a later question which relies upon this correct answer.

Determine

Use a graph, diagram, table or other element in the question to read a value for the quantity in the question.

Write down the answer

▶ with units

▶ to appropriate precision, i.e. the fewest number of significant figures in the question.

Other than reading the values for a particular point on a graph, you may need to

▶ calculate the gradient of the line

▶ calculate the gradient of a tangent to a curve

▶ calculate the area under a curve

▶ read the intercept value for the line with either the x- or the y-axis.

Sketch

Draw a sketch graph to show the shape of the relationship between the dependent and independent variables in the question.

▶ Axes must have labels with units.

▶ Axes must show the origin (as a zero).

▶ Axes may be labelled with any other relevant number as asked for in the question.

Be careful for asymptotic growth or decay curves – the line approaches but does not cross either axis, or maximum value line. If you know the relationship, then add it to the sketch

(for example, y varies as $\frac{1}{x^2}$).

Draw

Draw a graph with accurately plotted points, including a best-fit line, to show the shape of the relationship between the dependent and independent variables in the question.

▶ Axes must have labels with units.

▶ Axes must show the origin (as a zero).

▶ Axes must have a linear, uninterrupted scale.

▶ The best-fit line should pass through as many points as possible.

▶ The best-fit line may be a curve.

> **Top Tip!**
> If you are asked to calculate the gradient, data points must be taken from the best-fit line.

State (what is meant by)

Replicate or describe fully in your own words a definition of a physical term or phenomenon from the course specification document.

> For example, 'Knowledge that the threshold frequency is the minimum frequency of a photon required for photoemission' gives rise to the question 'State what is meant by threshold frequency.'

This is often the first part of a multi-part question and subsequent parts will contain related calculations. It is mainly recall. Try to keep to the precise definition.

Explain (what happens to …)

This is typically the latter part of a multi-part question. It may be asked as:

▶ 'State what happens to …'

▶ 'You must justify your answer.'

There is usually an equation which has been used previously in the question and which applies to the context.

▶ Write the equation down.
▶ Describe what is constant in the equation.
▶ Describe what has changed.
▶ Describe the effect of the change.

For example, 'The red laser is now replaced with a blue laser. Explain what happens to the interference pattern observed.'

▶ $m\lambda = d \sin \theta$
▶ λ has been increased
▶ m (the fringe order) and d (the slit spacing) remain constant
▶ therefore, θ must increase
▶ i.e. the fringe spacing becomes larger

Using your knowledge

This is typically an open-ended question stem worth 3 marks. If there is an obvious equation or relationship, write it down and/or sketch the graph. Describe the effect of changing the independent variable on the dependent variable within the question context.

There may be a number of acceptable answers depending upon the way in which you approach the problem.

Alternatively try to make three (bullet point) relevant comments about the context of the question.

Students aiming for a C grade should be able to attain 2 marks in this type of question.

Top Tip!

Marks are awarded on the basis of the level of understanding shown by your answer, overall, of the physics context:

• 'no' understanding (0 marks)
• 'limited' understanding (1 mark)
• 'reasonable' understanding (2 marks)
• 'good' understanding (3 marks).

Presenting numbers

Every time you give a number as a final answer, you must include the units and use the appropriate precision.

Units

Make sure that you use the correct unit following a calculation in your final answer. **If the unit is wrong or missing, you will lose the final mark!**

Significant figures

When calculating a value using an equation, take care not to give too many significant figures in your final answer. This means that the final answer can have no more significant figures than the value with the least number of significant figures used in the question.

Examples:

▶ 16·501 930 5 to 3 significant figures is 16·5
▶ 20 has 1 significant figure
▶ 40·0 has 3 significant figures
▶ 0·000 604 has 6 significant figures
▶ $4·30 \times 10^4$ has 3 significant figures
▶ 6200 has 2 significant figures

Scientific notation

When writing very large or very small numbers, use scientific notation to avoid writing or using strings of numbers in an answer or calculation.

Prefixes

You should be familiar with all common measurement prefixes, for example:

▶ nano (n) = $\times 10^{-9}$, 1 nm = 1×10^{-9} m = 0·000 000 001 m
▶ micro (μ) = $\times 10^{-6}$, 1 μm = 1×10^{-6} m = 0·000 001 m
▶ milli (m) = $\times 10^{-3}$, 1 mm = 1×10^{-3} m = 0·001 m
▶ kilo (k) = $\times 10^{3}$, 1 km = 1×10^{3} m = 1000 m
▶ mega (M) = $\times 10^{6}$, 1 Mm = 1×10^{6} m = 1 000 000 m
▶ giga (G) = $\times 10^{9}$, 1 Gm = 1×10^{9} m = 1 000 000 000 m

Top Tip!

Make sure you are familiar with how to enter and use numbers in scientific notation on your calculator before you sit your exam.

Our dynamic Universe

		MARK	STUDENT MARGIN
1	A radio-controlled drone was being used to survey an area of land. It flew 175 m due North, then 225 m on a bearing of 60° West of North. It took 2 minutes and 20 seconds to complete this journey.	4	Our dynamic Universe 1
a)	**(i)** Calculate the displacement of the drone during this flight. *Space for working and answer*		
	(ii) Calculate the average velocity of the drone during this flight. *Space for working and answer*	2	Our dynamic Universe 1
b)	The drone then flew directly back to its starting point in a further 1 minute 50 seconds. Calculate the average speed of the drone during the whole journey. *Space for working and answer*	3	Our dynamic Universe 1
		(9)	

MARKS | STUDENT MARGIN

2 A ball is dropped from a height of 1·75 m onto a laboratory floor.

a) **(i)** Calculate the time it takes to hit the ground.

Space for working and answer

3 | Our dynamic Universe 1

(ii) Calculate the velocity of the ball at the moment before it hits the ground.

Space for working and answer

3 | Our dynamic Universe 1

b) The ball then rebounds to a height of 1·23 m.

(i) Calculate the velocity of the ball at the moment it leaves the ground.

Space for working and answer

3 | Our dynamic Universe 1

(ii) Calculate the total time the ball takes to return to the floor after the first rebound.

Space for working and answer

3 | Our dynamic Universe 1

c) Use your answers to parts **a)** and **b)** to draw a velocity–time graph for the ball from when it is dropped until it reaches the ground for the second time.

3 | Our dynamic Universe 1

(15)

	MARKS	STUDENT MARGIN

3 A student is investigating the distance travelled by a projectile launched from a ramp. The angle of launch can be varied, as can the height h from which the projectile is released.

The projectile has a mass of 1·25 kg and is raised through a height of 1·4 m.

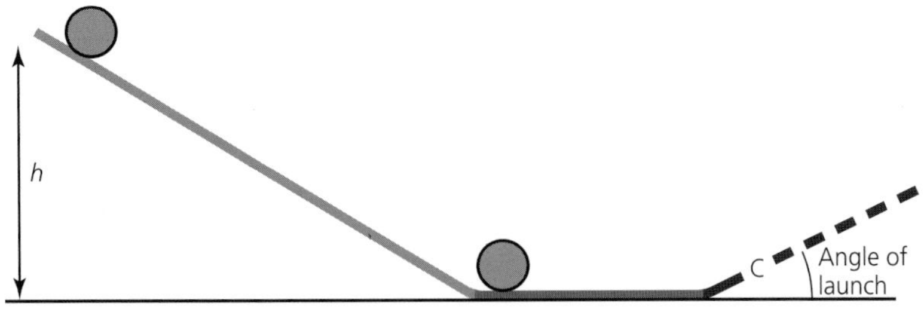

a) **(i)** Calculate the gain in potential energy of the projectile.

Space for working and answer

3 — Our dynamic Universe 2

(ii) Assuming no losses, calculate the velocity of the projectile during the horizontal section.

Space for working and answer

4 — Our dynamic Universe 2

b) The section at C in the diagram is used to change the angle of launch of the projectile and this is used in an experiment.

The velocity of the projectile as it left the launcher at an angle of 25° to the horizontal was measured as 4·5 m s^{-1}.

(i) Calculate the horizontal component of the velocity at launch.

Space for working and answer

1 — Our dynamic Universe 4

(ii) Calculate the vertical component of the velocity at launch.

Space for working and answer

1 — Our dynamic Universe 4

(iii) Calculate the horizontal distance travelled by the projectile at this angle.

Space for working and answer

4 — Our dynamic Universe 4

(iv) Sketch a graph showing how the horizontal velocity of the projectile varies with time until it hits the ground.

2 — Our dynamic Universe 1

(15)

17

		MARKS	STUDENT MARGIN

4 A theme park has a small train composed of an engine and three carriages. The mass of the engine and driver is 2750 kg and each carriage is 1450 kg.

The engine produces 6500 N of force when pulling the carriages.

a) Calculate the initial acceleration of the train.

Space for working and answer

4 — Our dynamic Universe 2

b) Calculate the tension in the coupling between the engine and the carriages as the train moves off.

Space for working and answer

2 — Our dynamic Universe 2

c) When operating, the train has a top speed of $2 \cdot 4\,\mathrm{m\,s^{-1}}$.

During one run the final carriage was removed from the train.

What effect would this have on the train's acceleration and top speed?

You must justify your answer.

2 — Our dynamic Universe 2

(8)

5 In satellite launches, multi-stage rockets are used to place the satellites in orbit around the Earth. The first stage takes the rocket to a certain height, it is jettisoned, and the second stage takes it further.

The details for an experimental prototype are:

Stage 1:

Mass of engine and casing = 3550 kg

Mass of fuel = 2740 kg

Thrust of engine = 120 000 N

Stage 2:

Mass of engine and casing = 1650 kg

Mass of fuel = 2150 kg

Thrust of engine = 105 000 N

a) Calculate the mass of the rocket at take-off.

Space for working and answer

1 — Our dynamic Universe 2

b) Calculate the initial acceleration of the rocket.

Space for working and answer

5 — Our dynamic Universe 2

		MARKS	STUDENT MARGIN

c) After the first stage has finished firing, the rocket is travelling at $1300\,\mathrm{m\,s^{-1}}$. The second-stage rocket ignites and fires for 25 seconds.

Assuming the stages have separated by this point, calculate the impulse applied to the second stage.

Space for working and answer

MARKS: 2   **STUDENT MARGIN:** Our dynamic Universe 3

d) In an earlier test launch, the first stage did not detach but the second-stage engine still managed to fire.

What difference would this have on the impulse given to the rocket?

MARKS: 1   **STUDENT MARGIN:** Our dynamic Universe 3

e) What difference would this make to the change in velocity of the rocket? You must justify your answer.

MARKS: 2   **STUDENT MARGIN:** Our dynamic Universe 3

(12)

6 A tanker is being towed by two tugboats, as shown in the diagram.

The mass of the tanker is $2 \cdot 84 \times 10^6\,\mathrm{kg}$. Each tug can exert a maximum force of $40 \cdot 0\,\mathrm{kN}$.

a) Calculate the magnitude of the resultant force applied by the combination of both tugs.

Space for working and answer

MARKS: 4   **STUDENT MARGIN:** Our dynamic Universe 2

b) Calculate the direction of the resultant force applied by the combination of both tugs.

Space for working and answer

MARKS: 3   **STUDENT MARGIN:** Our dynamic Universe 2

		MARKS	STUDENT MARGIN

c) Calculate the maximum acceleration of the tanker as a result of the towing force provided by the combination of both tugs.

Space for working and answer

MARKS: 3 — **STUDENT MARGIN:** Our dynamic Universe 2

d) In reality, the acceleration of the tanker will be less than the maximum acceleration calculated in part **c)**.

Explain why the actual acceleration is less than predicted (assume the answer in part **c)** was calculated correctly).

MARKS: 1 — **STUDENT MARGIN:** Our dynamic Universe 2

(11)

7 The Moon orbits the Earth, as shown in the diagram.

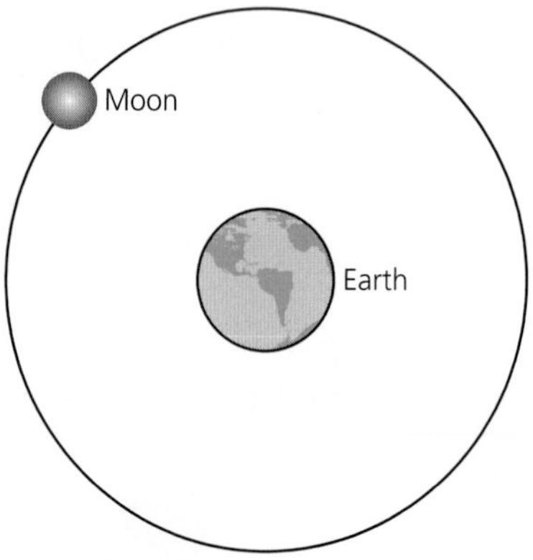

Data for the Moon–Earth orbit are as follows:

Mass of Moon (M_m): $7 \cdot 35 \times 10^{22}\,$kg

Mass of Earth (M_e): $5 \cdot 97 \times 10^{24}\,$kg

Orbit distance (R): $3 \cdot 85 \times 10^{5}\,$km

Orbit period: $27 \cdot 32$ days

a) Calculate the magnitude of the gravitational force between the Earth and the Moon.

Space for working and answer

MARKS: 3 — **STUDENT MARGIN:** Our dynamic Universe 4

b) State the vector direction of the gravitational force acting on the Moon.

MARKS: 1 — **STUDENT MARGIN:** Our dynamic Universe 4

c) A spacecraft is travelling from the Earth to the Moon.

The resultant gravitational force acting on the spacecraft is a vector combination of the force exerted by both the Earth and the Moon. At a particular distance, r_m, from the Moon, the resultant gravitational force will be zero.

Use the equation below to determine the value of r_m.

$$\sqrt{\frac{M_e}{M_m}} = \frac{R}{r_m} - 1$$

Space for working and answer

MARKS: 3 — **STUDENT MARGIN:** Our dynamic Universe 4

(7)

		MARKS	STUDENT MARGIN

8 When Hubble observed distant galaxies, he noted that all galaxies appeared to be moving away from our own galaxy. He found that distant galaxies were moving away from us at a greater velocity than galaxies that are closer to us.

Using your knowledge of physics, comment on these observations.

MARKS: 3 (3)

STUDENT MARGIN: Our dynamic Universe 6

9 When the NASA Moon missions were in operation, the command module orbited the Moon at a height of 190 km above the surface. The module had a mass of 28 400 kg.

The mass of the Moon is $7·34 \times 10^{22}$ kg.

The radius of the Moon is $1·74 \times 10^{6}$ m.

a) Calculate the gravitational force between the Moon and the command module.

Space for working and answer

MARKS: 5

STUDENT MARGIN: Our dynamic Universe 4

b) In a simulation, the NASA scientists considered what would happen if the command module rockets malfunctioned and reduced the orbital velocity to zero.

Explain what would happen to the command module under these conditions.

MARKS: 2 (7)

STUDENT MARGIN: Our dynamic Universe 4

10 In the 1970s, many car manufacturers tried to make their vehicles very rigid and able to survive a small collision with little or no deformation. Steering wheels and dashboards were made of toughened steel and aluminium.

Using your knowledge of physics, explain how changes in motor vehicle design and construction have made cars safer for drivers and passengers.

MARKS: 3 (3)

STUDENT MARGIN: Our dynamic Universe 3

	MARKS	STUDENT MARGIN

11 A star emits radiation across a range of wavelengths. The peak wavelength, λ_{peak}, is related to the surface temperature of the star by the formula

$$T = \frac{2 \cdot 898 \times 10^{-3}}{\lambda_{peak}}$$

a) A scientist reported that our Sun has a λ_{peak} of $5 \cdot 05 \times 10^{-9}$ m.
Calculate a value for the surface temperature of our Sun.
Space for working and answer

3 — Our dynamic Universe 6

b) The average temperature of space in our region is generally around $2 \cdot 0$ K.

(i) Calculate the peak wavelength of radiation associated with this temperature.
Space for working and answer

3 — Our dynamic Universe 6

(ii) What name is given to this radiation?
Explain why this supports the Big Bang theory of our Universe's existence.

3 — Our dynamic Universe 6

(9)

12 While studying distant galaxies, Hubble and others noted that all galaxies appear to be moving away from us. Furthermore, it was found that distant galaxies are moving away from us more rapidly. Data such as these were obtained from clusters in various galaxies:

Distance (light years)	Velocity (km/s)
$1 \cdot 00 \times 10^9$	$1 \cdot 50 \times 10^4$
$1 \cdot 40 \times 10^9$	$2 \cdot 20 \times 10^4$
$2 \cdot 50 \times 10^9$	$3 \cdot 90 \times 10^4$

a) Convert the distances in this table to m. You can use 1 year as $365 \cdot 25$ days.
Space for working and answer

3 — Our dynamic Universe 6

b) Convert the velocities in the table to m s^{-1}.
Space for working and answer

2 — Our dynamic Universe 6

| | | MARKS | STUDENT MARGIN |

c) Use the data to construct a graph of velocity versus distance and determine a value for Hubble's constant.

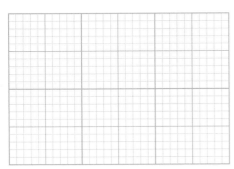

MARKS: **3**

STUDENT MARGIN: Our dynamic Universe 6

d) What possible value for the age of the Universe would this give?

Space for working and answer

MARKS: **2**

STUDENT MARGIN: Our dynamic Universe 6

(10)

Particles and waves

| | | MARKS | STUDENT MARGIN |

13 The kinetic energy distribution of the beta particles emitted by a ^{14}C radioactive source is shown below.

Note that $1 \cdot 0\,\text{MeV} = 1 \cdot 6 \times 10^{-13}\,\text{J}$.

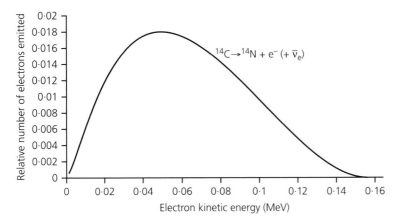

a) Explain why energy distributions such as these were used as the first evidence for the existence of the neutrino.

MARKS: **2**

STUDENT MARGIN: Particles and waves 2

b) Calculate the most common velocity of the beta particles emitted in this reaction.

Space for working and answer

MARKS: **4**

STUDENT MARGIN: Particles and waves 1

(6)

	MARKS	STUDENT MARGIN

14 A synchrotron is used to accelerate particles for scientific study. It uses a combination of electric and magnetic fields.

a) What is the purpose of the magnetic field?

1   Particles and waves 1

b) What is the purpose of the electric field?

1   Particles and waves 1

c) A proton, initially at rest, reaches an energy of 75 MeV.
Calculate the velocity of the proton at this energy.
Space for working and answer

4   Particles and waves 1

d) An improvement in the device is claimed to double the energy of particles within it. Explain what effect this improvement would have upon the velocity of the proton.

2   Particles and waves 1

(8)

15 A cyclotron (shown below) is used to accelerate protons.

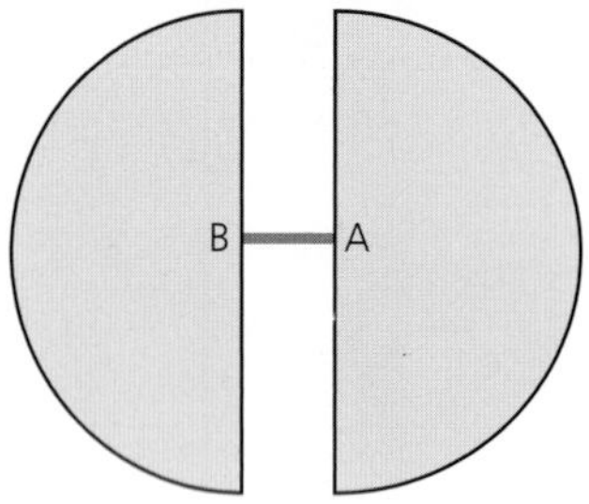

a) A proton at rest is accelerated across the gap from A to B at a voltage of 60 kV.
Calculate the velocity of the proton at point B.
Space for working and answer

4   Particles and waves 1

MARKS STUDENT MARGIN

b) Sketch an energy–time graph for the proton for the first four occasions it crosses the gap.

3 Particles and waves 1

(7)

16 Ion propulsion engines are efficient at propelling satellites through space. In a simplified example, xenon ions are accelerated from one end of an engine to the exhaust. The ions being ejected in one direction causes a force to be applied on the spacecraft in the opposite direction.

The spacecraft has a mass of 450 kg. The mass of a xenon ion is $2 \cdot 8 \times 10^{-25}$ kg, its charge is $1 \cdot 6 \times 10^{-19}$ C and it is accelerated through a voltage of $2 \cdot 5$ kV.

a) Calculate the gain in energy of a xenon ion as it travels through the electric field.

Space for working and answer

3 Particles and waves 1

b) Assuming the ion is initially at rest, calculate the speed of the ion as it leaves the engine.

Space for working and answer

3 Particles and waves 1

c) During a firing, $2 \cdot 0 \times 10^{-4}$ kg of xenon ions are ejected in 90 seconds. Calculate the average thrust this would generate.

Space for working and answer

3 Particles and waves 1

(9)

17 Both nuclear fusion and nuclear fission reactions can result in the release of energy.

a) Describe what is meant by fission.

3 Particles and waves 3

	MARKS	STUDENT MARGIN

b) Calculate the energy released in the following fusion reaction:

$$^{3}_{1}\text{H} + ^{3}_{1}\text{H} \rightarrow ^{4}_{2}\text{He} + 2\left(^{1}_{0}\text{n}\right)$$

Particle	Mass (kg)
$^{3}_{1}\text{H}$	$5{\cdot}00827 \times 10^{-27}$
$^{4}_{2}\text{He}$	$6{\cdot}64648 \times 10^{-27}$
$^{1}_{0}\text{n}$	$1{\cdot}67493 \times 10^{-27}$

Space for working and answer

4 — Particles and waves 3

c) Why are fusion reactors for power generation seen by some as a better alternative to fission reactors?

2 — Particles and waves 3

(9)

18 The diagram shows equipment used to investigate the photoelectric effect.

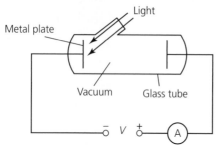

a) When green light is used to illuminate the target, no current flows.
What colour of visible light may be used to cause a current to be detected?
You must explain your answer.

3 — Particles and waves 5

b) The work function for the metal plate is $2{\cdot}8 \times 10^{-19}\,\text{J}$.
Calculate the minimum frequency of light which would cause a current to be detected.
Space for working and answer

3 — Particles and waves 5

(6)

	MARKS	STUDENT MARGIN

19 A laser is projected onto a diffraction grating, as shown.

The light has a wavelength of 565 nm.

The spacing of the grating $d = 3.5 \times 10^{-6}$ m.

Bright spots are seen on the screen, as shown.

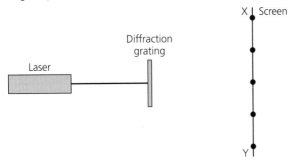

a) Calculate the angle between the central and the second order maximum.

Space for working and answer

4   Particles and waves 6

b) A light detector is moved between points X and Y.

Describe what it would register.

2   Particles and waves 6

(6)

20 Diamond has a relatively high refractive index of 2·42, which affects its critical angle and causes its 'sparkle' when illuminated with light.

a) State what is meant by critical angle.

1   Particles and waves 8

b) Calculate the critical angle for diamond.

Space for working and answer

3   Particles and waves 8

(4)

	MARKS	STUDENT MARGIN

21 A student investigates how irradiance, *I*, varies with distance, *d*, from a small lamp. The following apparatus is set up in a darkened laboratory.

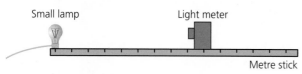

Small lamp   Light meter

Metre stick

a) State what is meant by irradiance.

1   Particles and waves 4

b) A graph of the student's data collected in this experiment is shown.
What further processing of the raw data is necessary in order to show a relationship of direct proportion between irradiance and distance?

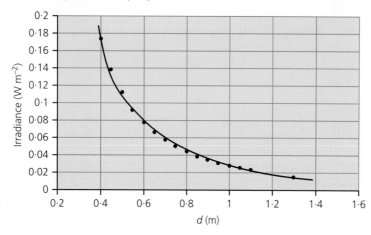

c) Explain why the experiment is carried out in a darkened laboratory.

1   Particles and waves 4

2   Particles and waves 4

(4)

22 Fraunhofer lines are any of the dark (absorption) lines in the spectrum of the Sun or other star. A typical spectrum of the light emitted by a star is shown. The absorptions labelled C, F, G and H correspond to specific wavelengths in the hydrogen atom emission spectrum.

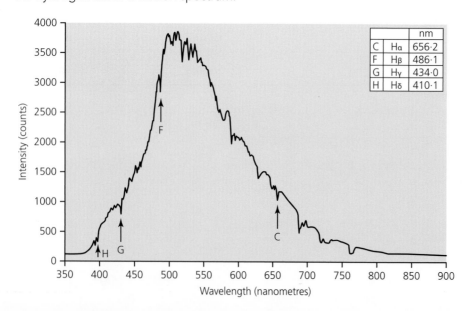

		nm
C	Hα	656·2
F	Hβ	486·1
G	Hγ	434·0
H	Hδ	410·1

	MARKS	STUDENT MARGIN

a) Explain why only specific wavelengths are observed to be missing from the star's spectrum.

MARKS: 2

STUDENT MARGIN: Particles and waves 7

b) For the hydrogen spectrum lines shown, calculate the minimum atomic electron energy transition associated with photons of these wavelengths.

Space for working and answer

MARKS: 4

STUDENT MARGIN: Particles and waves 7

(6)

Electricity

	MARKS	STUDENT MARGIN

23 A 12V lead/acid car battery is being used to test starter motors prior to them being fitted to car engines.

Thick copper connecting leads from the battery are attached to the motors and then they are switched on.

When not connected to the motors, the voltage across the battery is found to be 12·3V. When connected, the current from the battery is measured as 65A and the voltage across the battery is 9·2V.

a) Calculate the internal resistance of the battery.

Space for working and answer

MARKS: 3

STUDENT MARGIN: Electricity 3

b) When removing the leads from the motor, the technician accidentally allows the connecting clamps to glance off each other. This leads to a large spark being seen by the technician.

Suggest a reason why the spark is seen.

MARKS: 2

STUDENT MARGIN: Electricity 3

c) Why are thick leads used during these tests?

MARKS: 2

STUDENT MARGIN: Electricity 3

d) The same battery is used by the technician to charge a 220 mF capacitor and is connected in the circuit as shown.

How could the technician determine that the capacitor has been fully charged?

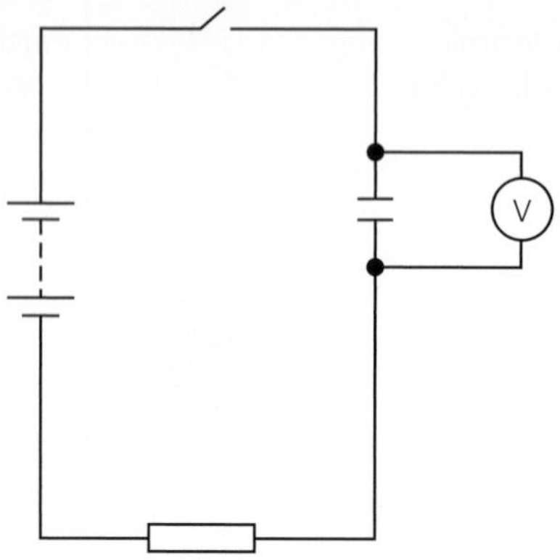

e) On another occasion the technician only has an ammeter for use.
How could this be used to determine when the capacitor is fully charged?

f) The capacitor is connected to a separate circuit with a component of resistance 85 Ω.
Calculate the initial current as the capacitor discharges.
Space for working and answer

g) This component is replaced with one of 225 Ω.
What effect would this have on the initial current and the time taken for the capacitor to discharge?

24 A student is investigating the following circuit.

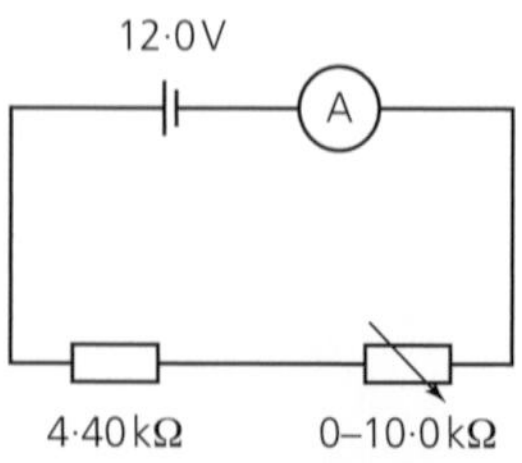

12·0V

A

4·40 kΩ   0–10·0 kΩ

a) Initially the ammeter shows a reading of 1·22 mA.
　　(i) Calculate the resistance of the variable resistor.
　　　　Space for working and answer

	MARKS	STUDENT MARGIN
d)	2	Electricity 4
e)	2	Electricity 4
f)	3	Electricity 4
g)	2	Electricity 4
	(16)	
a)(i)	4	Electricity 2

	MARKS	STUDENT MARGIN

    (ii) Calculate the voltage across the variable resistor.

         Space for working and answer

         3   Electricity 2

b) A 1·30 kΩ resistor is connected in parallel to the 4·40 kΩ resistor.

    (i) Calculate the total resistance of this pair of resistors connected in parallel.

        Space for working and answer

         3   Electricity 2

    (ii) What effect will this change have on the voltage across the variable resistor? You must justify your answer.

         Space for working and answer

         2   Electricity 2

(12)

25 A student is investigating batteries for use in a circuit.

One battery is rated 9 V. The student inserts it into a circuit as shown.

The student sets the resistance and measures the voltage and current. The resistance is altered and a number of readings are taken. These are shown in the following table.

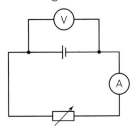

Voltage (V)	Current (A)
5·8	2·9
7·2	1·8
7·8	1·3
8·0	1·0

MARKS   STUDENT MARGIN

a)   Use these results to draw a graph of voltage against current.

4   Electricity 3

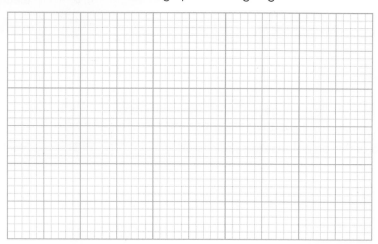

b)   Using this graph, determine:

    (i) the electromotive force (e.m.f.) of the battery;

1   Electricity 3

    (ii)   the internal resistance of the battery.

3   Electricity 3

(8)

Multiple-choice questions

Question	Answer	Mark
1	C	1
2	D	1
3	C	1
4	C	1
5	C	1
6	B	1
7	B	1
8	D	1
9	B	1
10	C	1
11	D	1
12	C	1
13	B	1
14	E	1
15	E	1
16	B	1
17	E	1
18	E	1
19	E	1

Question	Answer	Mark
20	E	1
21	D	1
22	A	1
23	E	1
24	C	1
25	C	1
26	C	1
27	D	1
28	D	1
29	A	1
30	A	1
31	A	1
32	D	1
33	B	1
34	B	1
35	A	1
36	D	1
37	D	1

Extended questions

Question			Answer		Marks
1	a)	(i)	$H = 225 \times \sin 60 = 194 \cdot 9\,\text{m (W)}$ $V = 225 \times \cos 60 = 112 \cdot 5\,\text{m (N)}$ (1) This gives a total of $175 + 112 \cdot 5 = 287 \cdot 5\,\text{m N}$ and $194 \cdot 9\,\text{m W}$ (1) $\text{Displacement} = \sqrt{287 \cdot 5^2 + 194 \cdot 9^2} = \sqrt{120\,642} = 347\,\text{m}$ (1) $\text{Direction} = \tan^{-1}\left(\dfrac{194 \cdot 9}{287 \cdot 5}\right) = 34^\circ\,\text{W}$ (1)		4
		(ii)	$\text{velocity} = \dfrac{\text{displacement}}{\text{time}}$ (1) $= \dfrac{347}{140}$ $= 2 \cdot 5\,\text{ms}^{-1}$ on a bearing of 326° (1)		2
	b)		$\text{speed} = \dfrac{\text{distance}}{\text{time}}$ (1) $= 175 + 225 + 347$ (1) $= \dfrac{747}{250} = 3 \cdot 0\,\text{ms}^{-1}$ (1)		3
					(9)
2	a)	(i)	$s = ut + \dfrac{1}{2}at^2$ and $u = 0$ (1) $s = \dfrac{1}{2}at^2$ $1 \cdot 75 = \dfrac{1}{2} \times 9 \cdot 8 \times t^2$ (1) $t^2 = \dfrac{1 \cdot 75 \times 2}{9 \cdot 8} = 0 \cdot 357$ $t = 0 \cdot 597 = 0 \cdot 60\,\text{s}$ (1)		3
		(ii)	$v = u + at$ (1) $v = 9 \cdot 8 \times 0 \cdot 6$ (1) $= 5 \cdot 9\,\text{ms}^{-1}$ (1)		3
	b)	(i)	$v^2 = u^2 + 2as$ $0 = u^2 + 2 \times -9 \cdot 8 \times 1 \cdot 23$ (1) $u^2 = 24 \cdot 108$ (1) $u = 4 \cdot 9\,\text{ms}^{-1}$ (1)		3

Question			Answer		Marks
		(ii)	Time to bounce up (and also to return)		3
			$v = u + at$; $0 = 4.9 - 9.8 \times t$	(1)	
			$t = \dfrac{4.9}{9.8} = 0.5$ s	(1)	
			Total time is $0.5 + 0.5 = 1.0$ s	(1)	
	c)				3
			Correct axes and scales	(1)	
			Correct units	(1)	
			Correct insertion of points and connecting line	(1)	
					(15)
3	a)	(i)	$E_p = m \times g \times h$	(1)	3
			$= 9.8 \times 1.25 \times 1.4 = 17.15$	(1)	
			$= 17$ J	(1)	
		(ii)	$17 = \frac{1}{2} \times m \times v^2$	(1)	4
			$17 = \frac{1}{2} \times 1.25 \times v^2$	(1)	
			$v^2 = \dfrac{34}{1.25} = 27.2$	(1)	
			$v = \sqrt{27.2} = 5.2\,\text{m s}^{-1}$	(1)	
	b)	(i)	$v_h = v \times \cos 25$		1
			$= 4.5 \times \cos 25 = 4.1\,\text{m s}^{-1}$		
		(ii)	$v_v = v \times \sin 25$		1
			$= 4.5 \times \sin 25 = 1.9\,\text{m s}^{-1}$		
		(iii)	$v = u + a \times t$	(1)	4
			$-1.9 = 1.9 + -9.8 \times t$	(1)	
			$t = \dfrac{-3.8}{-9.8}$	(1)	
			$= 0.388$ s	(1)	
			Horizontal distance is given by $v_h \times t = 4.1 \times 0.388 = 1.6$ m		
		(iv)			2
			Correct axes	(1)	
			Correct points	(1)	
					(15)

Question		Answer		Marks
4	a)	Mass of three carriages = $3 \times 1450 = 4350$ kg	(1)	4
		Mass of engine = 2750 kg	(1)	
		Total mass = 7100 kg		
		$a = \dfrac{F}{m}$	(1)	
		$= \dfrac{6500}{7100} = 0\cdot92$ m s^{-2}	(1)	
	b)	$F = m \times a$		2
		$= 4350 \times 0\cdot92$	(1)	
		$= 4002 = 4000$ N	(1)	
	c)	Less mass would result in a greater acceleration.	(1)	2
		This resultant drop in friction would also allow a greater top speed.	(1)	
				(8)
5	a)	Mass of rocket at take-off = $3550 + 2740 + 1650 + 2150 = 10090$ kg		1
	b)	$a = \dfrac{F}{m}$ where F is the unbalanced (resultant) force on the rocket	(1)	5
		$F = 120\,000$ N $-$ weight	(1)	
		Weight = $10\,090 \times 9\cdot8 = 98\,882$ N	(1)	
		$120\,000 - 98\,882 = 21\,118$ N	(1)	
		$a = \dfrac{21\,118}{10\,090}$		
		$= 2\cdot1$ m s^{-2}	(1)	
	c)	Impulse = $F \times t$	(1)	3
		$= 105\,000 \times 25$	(1)	
		$= 2\,625\,000$ N s	(1)	
	d)	It would make no difference to the impulse as this is due to the firing of the second-stage engine.		1
	e)	The change in velocity would be less (1) as the mass of the rocket is greater due to the first stage not being ejected (1).		2
				(12)
6	a)	In the XY direction		4
		Tug 1:		
		$F = 40\cdot0 \times 10^3 \times \cos(25) = 3\cdot63 \times 10^4$		
		Tug 2:		
		$F = 40\cdot0 \times 10^3 \times \cos(-15) = 3\cdot86 \times 10^4$		
		Total = $7\cdot49 \times 10^4$ N *to the right*	(1)	
		Perpendicular to XY		
		Tug 1:		
		$F = 40\cdot0 \times 10^3 \times \sin(25) = 1\cdot69 \times 10^4$		
		Tug 2:		
		$F = 40\cdot0 \times 10^3 \times \sin(-15) = -1\cdot04 \times 10^4$		
		Total = $6\cdot5 \times 10^3$ N *up the page*	(1)	
		Pythagoras gives resultant magnitude:		
		$F = \sqrt{[(7\cdot49^2 + 0\cdot65^2) \times 10^8]}$	(1)	
		$F = 7\cdot518 \times 10^4$ N		
		$F = 7\cdot52 \times 10^4$ N	(1)	

Question		Answer		Marks
	b)	$\tan \theta = \dfrac{\text{perpendicular}}{\text{parallel}}$ (1) $\tan \theta = \dfrac{6 \cdot 5 \times 10^3}{7 \cdot 52 \times 10^4}$ (1) $\theta = \tan^{-1}(8 \cdot 6436 \times 10^{-2})$ $\theta = 4 \cdot 94°$ above the line XY (1)		3
	c)	$F = ma$ (1) $7 \cdot 52 \times 10^4 = 2 \cdot 84 \times 10^6 \times a$ (1) $a = 2 \cdot 6479 \times 10^{-2}\,\text{m s}^{-2}$ $a = 2 \cdot 65 \times 10^{-2}\,\text{m s}^{-2}$ at $4 \cdot 94°$ above the line XY (1)		3
	d)	Other resistive/frictional forces will act on both tug and tanker to oppose the forward motion.		1
				(11)
7	a)	$F = \dfrac{Gm_1 m_2}{r^2}$ (1) $F = \dfrac{6 \cdot 67 \times 10^{-11} \times 5 \cdot 97 \times 10^{24} \times 7 \cdot 35 \times 10^{22}}{(3 \cdot 85 \times 10^8)^2}$ (1) $F = 1 \cdot 9745 \times 10^{20}\,\text{N}$ $F = 1 \cdot 97 \times 10^{20}\,\text{N}$ (1)		3
	b)	The force acts along the vector connecting the centre of mass of the Moon and the centre of mass of the Earth (i.e. along the radius vector).		1
	c)	$\sqrt{\dfrac{M_e}{M_m}} = \dfrac{R}{r_m} - 1$ (1) $\sqrt{\dfrac{5 \cdot 97 \times 10^{24}}{7 \cdot 35 \times 10^{22}}} = \dfrac{3 \cdot 85 \times 10^8}{r_m} - 1$ (1) $r_m = \dfrac{3 \cdot 85 \times 10^8}{9 \cdot 0125 + 1}$ $r_m = 3 \cdot 8452 \times 10^7\,\text{m}$ $r_m = 3 \cdot 85 \times 10^7\,\text{m}$ (1)		3
				(7)
8		**Sample answer** ▸ Hubble found a relationship of direct proportion between the distance from Earth of an observed galaxy and the velocity of the galaxy. Distances (d) were calculated using the parallax method and velocities (v) were calculated using Doppler redshift observations. ▸ Graphing this data gave a best-fit line with constant gradient which passed through the origin of the graph and allowed Hubble to propose that a law existed such that $v = Hd$, where H is the gradient of the line, i.e. the constant of proportionality. This constant has dimensions of $\dfrac{1}{\text{time}}$ and so may be used to estimate the age of the Universe, where age $= \dfrac{1}{H}$. ▸ In addition, the fact that all galaxies are moving away from each other and that the more distant ones are moving more quickly leads to a thought experiment of 'reversing time' – playing the expanding Universe backwards suggests that all galaxies originated from a single point and gives rise to the possibility of a 'Big Bang' theory of a single point of Universe origin.		3
				(3)

Question		Answer		Marks
9	a)	$r = 1 \cdot 74 \times 10^6 + 1 \cdot 90 \times 10^5$		5
		$r = 1 \cdot 93 \times 10^6 \, \text{m}$	(1)	
		$r^2 = 3 \cdot 72 \times 10^{12}$	(1)	
		$F = G\dfrac{m_1 m_2}{r^2}$	(1)	
		$F = \dfrac{(6 \cdot 67 \times 10^{-11} \times 7 \cdot 34 \times 10^{22} \times 28\,400)}{3 \cdot 72 \times 10^{12}}$	(1)	
		$F = 37\,376 \, \text{N} = 37\,400 \, \text{N}$	(1)	
	b)	The module would be attracted by the gravitational field of the Moon.	(1)	2
		With no orbital velocity, it would gradually accelerate towards the surface of the Moon.	(1)	
				(7)
10		**Sample answer**		3
		▸ Early cars were made to be strong and sturdy and not easily damaged. This resulted in serious injury for drivers and passengers as they made contact with the vehicle during collisions.		
		▸ Softer materials, air bags and crumple zones are designed to reduce the rate at which the passenger is slowed down. They do this by increasing the time taken for the vehicle to stop. Crumple zones absorb energy and stop the car over a longer time. Air bags inflate and reduce the speed of the passenger gradually.		
		▸ If the passenger strikes the dashboard it will be curved (not sharp) and have a degree of padding. All of this is intended to decrease the rate at which the passenger slows down, therefore reducing the force on impact.		
				(3)
11	a)	$T = \dfrac{2 \cdot 898 \times 10^{-3}}{\lambda_{peak}}$	(1)	3
		$= \dfrac{2 \cdot 898 \times 10^{-3}}{5 \cdot 05 \times 10^{-9}}$	(1)	
		$= 5 \cdot 74 \times 10^5 \, \text{K}$	(1)	
	b) (i)	$T = \dfrac{2 \cdot 898 \times 10^{-3}}{\lambda_{peak}}$	(1)	3
		$\lambda_{peak} = \dfrac{2 \cdot 898 \times 10^{-3}}{2 \cdot 0}$	(1)	
		$= 0 \cdot 001\,449 = 1 \cdot 45 \times 10^{-3} \, \text{m}$	(1)	
	(ii)	This is in the microwave radiation band (1). It was proposed that this radiation would be present as a result of the expansion of the Universe (1) and when it was detected, it provided very strong evidence in support of the Big Bang theory (1).		3
				(9)

Question		Answer	Marks
12	a)	To convert light years to m you multiply the distance (ly) by $365 \cdot 25 \times 24 \times 60 \times 60 \times 3 \times 10^8$ (1) e.g. $1 \cdot 40 \times 10^9$ ly becomes 133×10^{25} m (1) Distances are (m): $9 \cdot 47 \times 10^{24}$ $1 \cdot 33 \times 10^{25}$ $2 \cdot 37 \times 10^{25}$ (1)	3
	b)	Velocities are (m s^{-1}): $1 \cdot 50 \times 10^7$ $2 \cdot 20 \times 10^7$ $3 \cdot 90 \times 10^7$ No errors: 2 marks One or two errors: 1 mark Three errors: 0 marks	2
	c)	 Gradient $m = \dfrac{(y_2 - y_1)}{(x_2 - x_1)}$ (1) $= \dfrac{(3 \cdot 90 - 1 \cdot 50) \times 10^7}{2 \cdot 37 \times 10^{25} - 9 \cdot 47 \times 10^{24}}$ $= 1 \cdot 686 \times 10^{-18}$ (1) $H_0 = 1 \cdot 69 \times 10^{-18} \, \text{s}^{-1}$ (1)	3
	d)	Time $= \dfrac{1}{H_0}$ (1) $= \dfrac{1}{1 \cdot 69 \times 10^{-18}}$ $= 5 \cdot 92 \times 10^{17}$ s (1)	2
			(10)
13	a)	The nuclear decay is a quantum process and so always involves the same energy change. (1) If the beta particle has a range of energies then there must be another, difficult to detect (low mass and uncharged) particle, i.e. the neutrino. (1)	2

39

Question		Answer	Marks
	b)	From the graph, most common energy is $0.05\,\text{MeV}$.	**4**
		$E_k = 0.05 \times 1.6 \times 10^{-13}\,\text{J}$	
		$E_k = 8.0 \times 10^{-15}\,\text{J}$	(1)
		$E_k = \dfrac{1}{2}mv^2$	(1)
		$80 \times 10^{-15} = \dfrac{1}{2} \times 9.11 \times 10^{-31} \times v^2$	(1)
		$v = \sqrt{\left(\dfrac{16 \times 10^{-15}}{9.11 \times 10^{-31}}\right)}$	
		$v = 1.3253 \times 10^8\,\text{m s}^{-1}$	
		$v = 1.3 \times 10^8\,\text{m s}^{-1}$	(1)
			(6)
14	**a)**	To direct the particles and to ensure they follow the correct path	**1**
	b)	To accelerate the particles	**1**
	c)	$E = 75\,\text{MeV}$	**4**
		$\quad = 75 \times 10^6 \times 1.6 \times 10^{-19}\,\text{J}$	
		$\quad = 1.2 \times 10^{-11}\,\text{J}$	(1)
		$E_k = \dfrac{1}{2} \times m \times v^2$	(1)
		$1.2 \times 10^{-11} = \dfrac{1}{2} \times 1.673 \times 10^{-27} \times v^2$	(1)
		$v^2 = \dfrac{2 \times 1.2 \times 10^{-11}}{1.673 \times 10^{-27}}$	
		$\quad = 1.43 \times 10^{16}$	
		$v = 1.2 \times 10^8\,\text{m s}^{-1}$	(1)
	d)	Energy varies as the square of velocity.	(1) **2**
		Doubling energy will increase velocity by a factor of $\sqrt{2}$, i.e. 1.4 times greater.	(1)
			(8)
15	**a)**	$E = q \times V$	**4**
		$E = 1.6 \times 10^{-19} \times 60\,000$	
		$\quad = 9.6 \times 10^{-15}\,\text{J}$	(1)
		$E_k = \dfrac{1}{2} \times m \times v^2$	(1)
		$9.6 \times 10^{-15} = \dfrac{1}{2} \times 1.673 \times 10^{-27} \times v^2$	(1)
		$v^2 = \dfrac{2 \times 9.6 \times 10^{-15}}{1.673 \times 10^{-27}}$	
		$v^2 = 1.147 \times 10^{13}$	
		$v = 3.4 \times 10^6\,\text{m s}^{-1}$	(1)

Question		Answer		Marks
	b)	Axes (1) Graph with: horizontal (1) sloping steps (1)		3
				(7)
16	a)	$E = qV$ (1) $\quad = 1\cdot6 \times 10^{-19} \times 2500$ (1) $\quad = 4\cdot0 \times 10^{-16}\,\text{J}$ (1)		3
	b)	$E = \dfrac{1}{2}mv^2$ (1) $4\cdot0 \times 10^{-16} = \dfrac{1}{2} \times 2\cdot8 \times 10^{-25} \times v^2$ $v^2 = \dfrac{2 \times 4\cdot0 \times 10^{-16}}{2\cdot8 \times 10^{-25}}$ (1) $v^2 = 2\cdot857 \times 10^9$ $v = 5\cdot3 \times 10^4\,\text{m s}^{-1}$ (1)		3
	c)	$F \times \Delta t = m \times \Delta v$ (1) $F \times 90 = 0\cdot0002 \times 5\cdot3 \times 10^4$ (1) $F = \dfrac{0\cdot0002 \times 5\cdot3 \times 10^4}{90} = 0\cdot118 = 0\cdot12\,\text{N}$ (1)		3
				(9)
17	a)	In a fission reaction more massive nuclei are separated or 'split' to form smaller nuclei. (1) The total mass of the smaller nuclei is less than that of the original nucleus. (1) This 'excess' mass is converted to energy and is used to generate electricity in power stations. (1)		3
	b)	Mass before reaction $= 5\cdot008\,27 \times 10^{-27} + 5\cdot008\,27 \times 10^{-27} = 1\cdot001\,654 \times 10^{-26}\,\text{kg}$ Mass after reaction $= 6\cdot646\,48 \times 10^{-27} + 2 \times 1\cdot674\,93 \times 10^{-27} = 9\cdot996\,34 \times 10^{-27}\,\text{kg}$ Difference in mass $= 2\cdot02 \times 10^{-29}\,\text{kg}$ (1) Energy $= m \times c^2$ (1) $\quad = 2\cdot02 \times 10^{-29} \times (3 \times 10^8)^2$ (1) $\quad = 1\cdot818 \times 10^{-12}\,\text{J}$ $\quad = 1\cdot82 \times 10^{-12}\,\text{J}$ (1)		4
	c)	In a fusion reaction there is less radioactive waste. (1) This means there are fewer issues associated with decontamination and storage of low-level waste. (1)		2
				(9)

Question		Answer		Marks
18	a)	Any wavelength shorter then green (e.g. blue, violet, UV).	(1)	3
		This will mean the frequency is higher and so the energy of each photon ($E = hf$) is larger.	(1)	
		If the photon energy is larger than the work function, a current will be detected.	(1)	
	b)	$E = hf$	(1)	3
		$2 \cdot 8 \times 10^{-19} = 6 \cdot 63 \times 10^{-34} \times f$	(1)	
		$f = 4 \cdot 2232 \times 10^{14}\,\text{Hz}$		
		$f = 4 \cdot 2 \times 10^{14}\,\text{Hz}$	(1)	
				(6)
19	a)	$d \sin \theta = m\lambda$	(1)	4
		$\sin \theta = \dfrac{m\lambda}{d}$	(1)	
		$= \dfrac{2 \times 565 \times 10^{-9}}{3 \cdot 5 \times 10^{-6}}$		
		$= 0 \cdot 323$	(1)	
		$= 18 \cdot 8° = 19°$	(1)	
	b)	As the detector moves from X to Y it will cut across five 'lines' of constructive interference (including the central maximum)	(1)	2
		and four 'lines' of destructive interference.	(1)	
				(6)
20	a)	As a wave moves from a more dense to a less dense medium, the critical angle is the minimum incident angle beyond which total internal reflection takes place.		1
	b)	$\sin \theta_c = \dfrac{1}{n}$	(1)	3
		$\sin \theta_c = \dfrac{1}{2 \cdot 42}$	(1)	
		$\theta_c = \sin^{-1}\left(\dfrac{1}{2 \cdot 42}\right)$		
		$\theta_c = 24 \cdot 407$		
		$\theta_c = 24 \cdot 4°$	(1)	
				(4)
21	a)	Irradiance is the power of the source per unit area.		1
	b)	Given the relationship $I = \dfrac{k}{d^2}$, the data need to be processed to calculate $\dfrac{1}{d^2}$.	(1)	2
		A graph of I vs $\dfrac{1}{d^2}$ will be a straight line through the origin (i.e. directly proportional).	(1)	
	c)	Stray light from the room would affect the results; the graph of I vs $\dfrac{1}{d^2}$ would not pass through the origin because of this systematic error (uncertainty).		1
				(4)

Question			Answer		Marks
22	a)		The light emitted by a star is a continuous spectrum.	(1)	2
			As that light passes through the gases in the atmosphere of the star, specific wavelengths are absorbed by the atoms/molecules of gas.	(1)	
	b)		$f = \dfrac{3 \times 10^8}{656 \cdot 2 \times 10^9}$	(1)	4
			$E = hf$	(1)	
			$E = \dfrac{6 \cdot 63 \times 10^{-34} \times 3 \times 10^8}{656 \cdot 2 \times 10^{-9}}$	(1)	
			$E = 3 \cdot 03109 \times 10^{-19}\,\mathrm{J}$		
			$E = 3 \cdot 031 \times 10^{-19}\,\mathrm{J}$	(1)	
					(6)
23	a)		Lost volts $= Ir$		3
			$\quad 31 = 65 \times r$	(1)	
			$r = \dfrac{3 \cdot 1}{65}$	(1)	
			$\quad = 0 \cdot 048 = 0 \cdot 05\,\Omega$	(1)	
	b)		When the leads touch, they are effectively short circuiting the battery. This means that all the voltage is across the internal resistance of the battery.	(1)	2
			This produces a very high current $I = \dfrac{E}{r} = \dfrac{12 \cdot 3}{0 \cdot 05} = 246\text{ A}.$ This can generate the sparks.	(1)	
	c)		With a normal operating current of 65 A, a thin cable would overheat.	(1)	2
			In order to survive such high loads, a thick cable is required.	(1)	
	d)		Observe the reading on the voltmeter	(1)	2
			and when voltage across capacitor reaches a constant value, the capacitor is fully charged.	(1)	
	e)		Connect the ammeter in series with the capacitor and switch on.	(1)	2
			When ammeter reading drops to zero, the capacitor is fully charged.	(1)	
	f)		$I = \dfrac{V}{R}$	(1)	3
			$\quad = \dfrac{12 \cdot 3}{85}$	(1)	
			$\quad = 0 \cdot 14\text{ A}$	(1)	
	g)		The initial current would be smaller as there is a larger resistance in the circuit.	(1)	2
			The smaller current would mean it would take longer to discharge.	(1)	
					(16)
24	a)	(i)	$V = \dfrac{I}{R_{\text{total}}}$	(1)	4
			$12 \cdot 0 = 1 \cdot 22 \times 10^{-3} \times R_{\text{total}}$	(1)	
			$R_{\text{total}} = 9836$		
			$R_{\text{var}} = 9836 - 4400$	(1)	
			$R_{\text{var}} = 5436\,\Omega = 5440\,\Omega$	(1)	

Question			Answer		Marks
		(ii)	$V = \dfrac{I}{R}$	(1)	3
			$V = 1{\cdot}22 \times 10^{-3} \times 5440$	(1)	
			$V = 6{\cdot}637 = 6{\cdot}64\,\text{V}$	(1)	
	b)	(i)	$\dfrac{1}{R_T} = \dfrac{1}{R_1} + \dfrac{1}{R_2}$	(1)	3
			$= \dfrac{1}{4400} + \dfrac{1}{1300} = 9.965 \times 10^{-4}$	(1)	
			$R_T = 1003 = 1000\,\Omega$	(1)	
		(ii)	This will increase the voltage across the variable resistor. The resistance of the parallel resistors will be less than $4400\,\Omega$.	(1)	2
			There will be less voltage across this section. Therefore, more voltage across the variable resistor.	(1)	
					(12)
25	a)				4
			Axes and units appropriately scaled	(1)	
			y-axis: voltage going up to 10 V	(1)	
			x-axis: current going up to 4 A	(1)	
			Correct plotting of all points and best-fit line drawn	(1)	
	b)	(i)	Extend graph to intersect y-axis to give $E = 9{\cdot}0\,\text{V}$ (accept 8·7V to 9·3V)		1
		(ii)	Calculate gradient of graph to determine internal resistance	(1)	3
			$m = \dfrac{(y_2 - y_1)}{(x_2 - x_1)}$		
			$= \dfrac{(8.0 - 5.8)}{(1.0 - 2.9)}$		
			$= \dfrac{2.2}{-1.9} = -1.2$	(1)	
			The gradient of the graph is $-r = -1{\cdot}2$		
			therefore $r = 1{\cdot}2\,\Omega$	(1)	
					(8)

Duration: 3 hours
Total marks: 155

PAPER 1 – 25 marks
Attempt ALL questions.

PAPER 2 – 130 marks
Attempt ALL questions.

Reference may be made to the Relationships sheet on page xi and to the Data sheet on page xiii.

Care should be taken to give an appropriate number of significant figures in the final answers to calculations.

Write your answers clearly in the spaces provided in this paper. Any rough work must be written in this paper. You should score through your rough work when you have written your final copy.

Use **blue** or **black** ink.

Paper 1

Total marks: 25
Duration: 45 minutes
Attempt ALL questions.

	MARKS	STUDENT MARGIN

1   The following velocity–time graph represents the motion of a car travelling in a straight line.

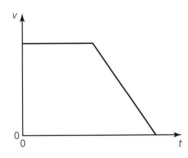

Which of the following displacement–time graphs represents the same motion?

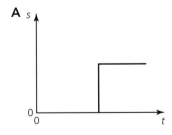

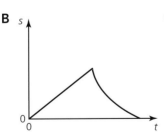

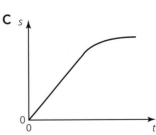

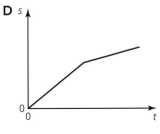

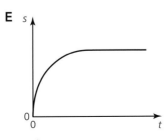

MARKS: 1

STUDENT MARGIN: Our dynamic Universe 1

	MARKS	STUDENT MARGIN

2 An object is accelerating at $5{\cdot}0\,m\,s^{-2}$. — **1** — Our dynamic Universe 1

This means that the

A distance travelled by the object increases by 5 metres every second

B displacement of the object increases by 5 metres every second

C speed of the object is $5\,m\,s^{-1}$ every second

D velocity of the object is $5\,m\,s^{-1}$ every second

E velocity of the object increases by $5\,m\,s^{-1}$ every second.

3 A vehicle is travelling in a straight line. Graphs of velocity and acceleration against time are shown below. — **1** — Our dynamic Universe 1

Which pair of graphs could represent the motion of the vehicle?

A

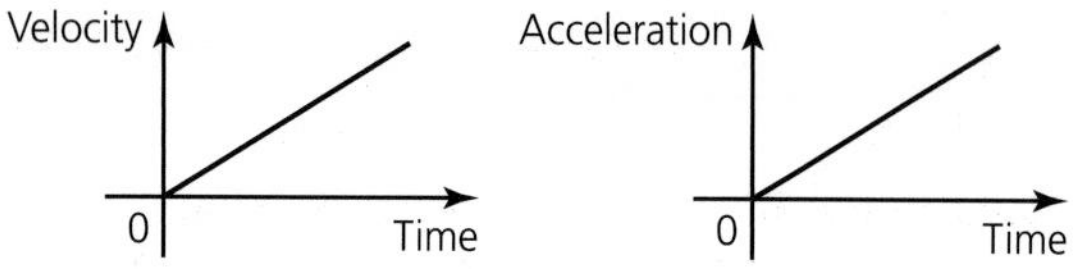

B

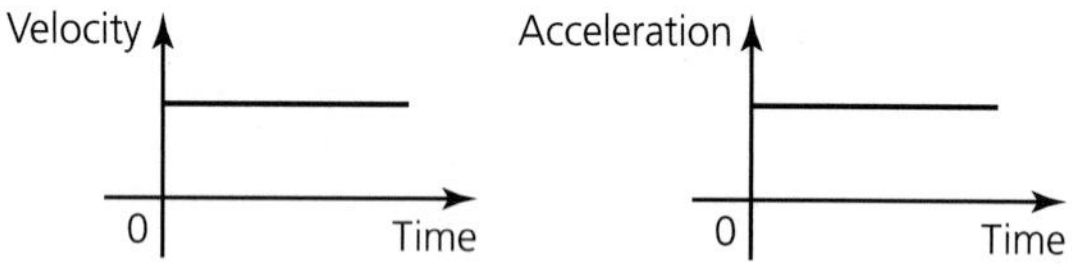

C

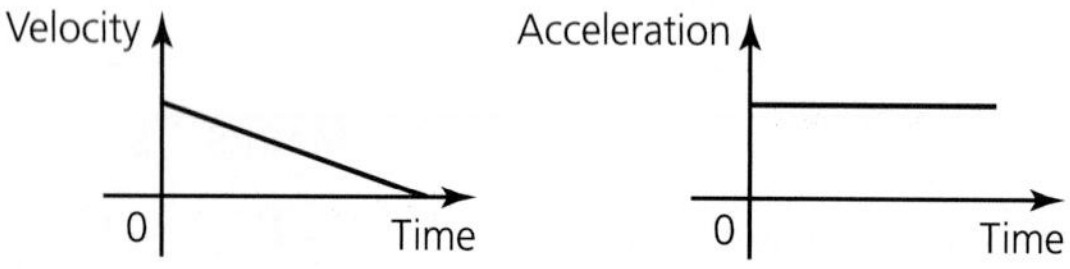

D

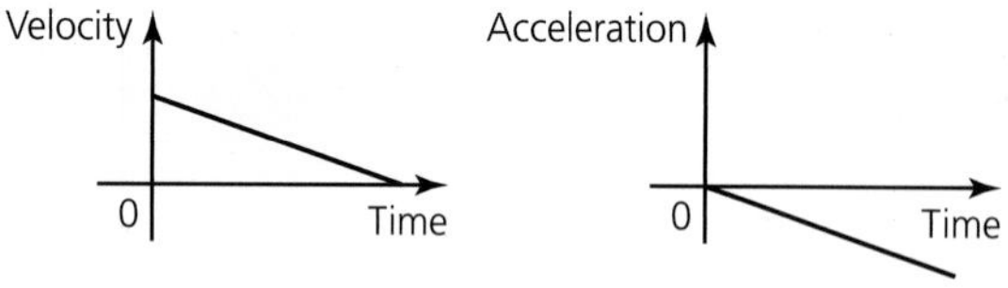

E

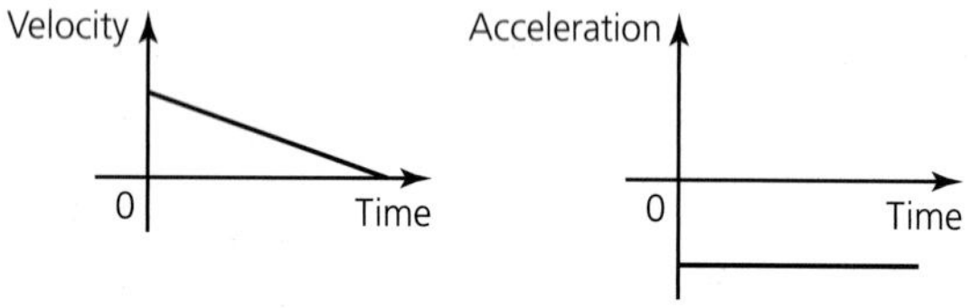

4 A model helicopter flies with constant velocity at constant height. — **1** — Our dynamic Universe 2

Which diagram represents the forces acting on the helicopter?

A

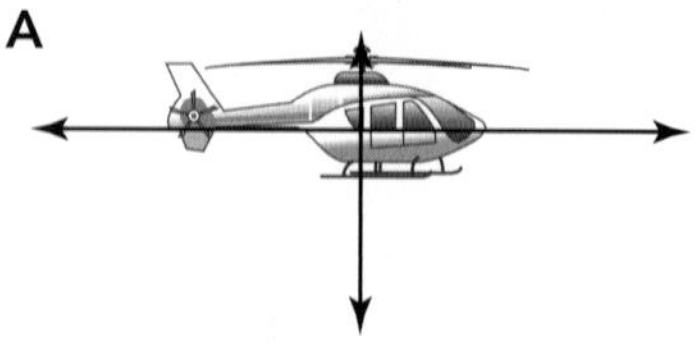

B

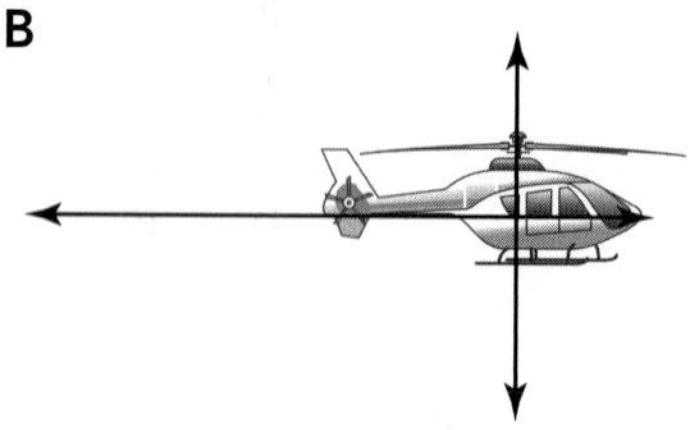

C

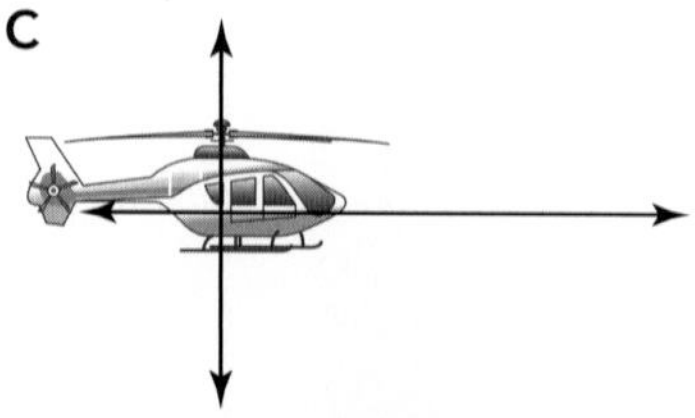

D

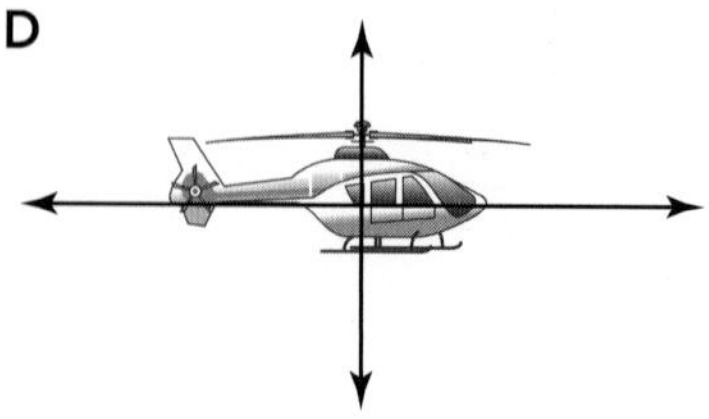

E

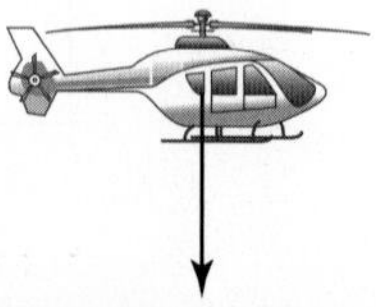

MARKS | STUDENT MARGIN

5 An object of mass *m* is at rest on a slope.

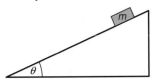

Which row of the table correctly shows the components of weight acting down and normal to the slope?

	Component down the slope	Component normal to the slope
A	$mg \tan \theta$	$mg \cos \theta$
B	$mg \sin \theta$	$mg \tan \theta$
C	$mg \sin \theta$	$mg \cos \theta$
D	$mg \cos \theta$	$mg \sin \theta$
E	$mg \cos \theta$	$mg \tan \theta$

1 — Our dynamic Universe 2

6 Two trolleys collide and stick together as shown.

Initially, trolley A is moving at $0.60\,\mathrm{m\,s^{-1}}$. It collides with and sticks to stationary trolley B. The trolleys move off together as shown, at $0.30\,\mathrm{m\,s^{-1}}$.

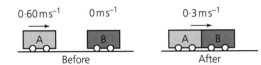

How do the masses of the trolleys compare?

A Trolley A has two times the mass of trolley B.
B Trolley B has two times the mass of trolley A.
C Trolley A has the same mass as trolley B.
D Trolley A has four times the mass of trolley B.
E Trolley B has four times the mass of trolley A.

1 — Our dynamic Universe 3

7 A satellite orbits a planet at a distance of $3.0 \times 10^7\,\mathrm{m}$ from the centre of the planet. The mass of the satellite is $1.8 \times 10^4\,\mathrm{kg}$. The mass of the planet is $4.2 \times 10^{24}\,\mathrm{kg}$.

The gravitational force acting on the satellite due to the planet is

A $8.4 \times 10^{13}\,\mathrm{N}$
B $1.7 \times 10^{11}\,\mathrm{N}$
C $5.6 \times 10^3\,\mathrm{N}$
D $1.7 \times 10^3\,\mathrm{N}$
E $8.4 \times 10^{-3}\,\mathrm{N}$.

1 — Our dynamic Universe 4

8 Which of the following provide evidence for dark energy?
I The distance–age relationship of observed galaxies.
II The mass–rotational speed relationship of observed galaxies.
III The expansion rate–time relationship of the Universe.

A I only
B II only
C III only
D I and II only
E I and III only

1 — Our dynamic Universe 6

9   The graph shows how the energy emitted per second from the surface of a hot object varies with the wavelength, λ, of the emitted radiation at different temperatures.

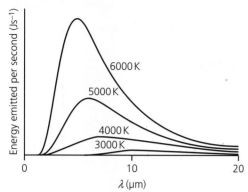

A student makes the following statements based on the information shown in the graph.

I   As the temperature of the object increases, the total energy emitted per second increases.

II   As the temperature of the object decreases, the peak wavelength of the emitted radiation increases.

III   The frequency of the emitted radiation steadily increases as the emitted energy per second decreases.

Which of the statements is/are correct?

A   I only

B   II only

C   III only

D   I and II only

E   II and III only

1

Our dynamic Universe 6

10   Which of the following lists the particles in order of size from smallest to largest?

A   helium nucleus; electron; proton

B   helium nucleus; proton; electron

C   proton; helium nucleus; electron

D   electron; helium nucleus; proton

E   electron; proton; helium nucleus

1

Particles and waves 2

11   Which of the following are fermions?

I   quarks

II   leptons

III   neutrinos

A   I only

B   II only

C   III only

D   I and II only

E   I, II and III

1

Particles and waves 2

| | MARKS | STUDENT MARGIN |

12 Which of the following are bosons?

   I   photons

   II   leptons

   III gluons

   A   I only

   B   II only

   C   III only

   D   I and II only

   E   I and III only

1 — Particles and waves 2

13 Radioactive beta decay gave the first evidence of the existence of the neutrino because

   A   the charge of the emitted particle is not constant

   B   the kinetic energy of the emitted particle is not constant

   C   the mass of the emitted particle is not constant

   D   the spin of the emitted particle is not constant

   E   the size of the emitted particle is not constant.

1 — Particles and waves 2

14 Which row of the table correctly shows the charge on the particles for the electric field patterns shown below?

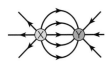

	Charge X	Charge Y	Charge Z
A	positive	negative	negative
B	positive	negative	positive
C	negative	positive	negative
D	positive	positive	negative
E	negative	negative	positive

1 — Particles and waves 1

15 The definition of the volt is

   A   the work done moving unit charge between two points

   B   the work done moving unit charge outside the electric field

   C   half the energy stored per unit charge in a capacitor

   D   the square root of energy divided by capacitance

   E   half the square root of energy divided by capacitance.

1 — Particles and waves 1

16 A proton enters a magnetic field as shown in the diagram.

Which of the following describes the effect of the field on the proton's velocity vector?

   A   The magnitude of the velocity vector increases.

   B   The magnitude of the velocity vector decreases.

   C   The direction of the velocity vector changes towards the top of the field.

   D   The direction of the velocity vector changes towards the bottom of the field.

   E   The direction of the velocity vector changes to move out of the page.

1 — Particles and waves 1

	MARKS	STUDENT MARGIN

17 In a particle accelerator, which of the following statements is/are true?

    I Electric fields are used to accelerate particles in a straight line.

    II Magnetic fields are used to accelerate particles in a straight line.

    III Gravitational fields are used to accelerate particles in a straight line.

    A I only

    B II only

    C III only

    D I and II only

    E I and III only

1 — Particles and waves 1

18 In the following nuclear decay, identify the missing particle X.

$$^{23}_{12}\mathrm{Mg} \rightarrow {}^{23}_{11}\mathrm{Na} + \mathrm{X} + {}^{0}_{0}v$$

    A electron

    B positron

    C proton

    D electron neutrino

    E positron neutrino

1 — Particles and waves 3

19 What is meant when two wave sources are described as coherent?

    A The path difference between the two sources is constant.

    B The irradiance of the two sources is constant.

    C The amplitude of the two sources is fixed.

    D The frequency difference between the two sources is constant.

    E The phase difference between the two sources is constant.

1 — Particles and waves 6

20 For the ray diagram below, which is the correct definition of refractive index, n?

1 — Particles and waves 8

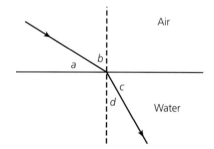

    A $n = \dfrac{\sin a}{\sin c}$

    B $n = \dfrac{\sin a}{\sin d}$

    C $n = \dfrac{\sin b}{\sin c}$

    D $n = \dfrac{\sin b}{\sin d}$

    E $n = \dfrac{1}{\sin a}$

	MARKS	STUDENT MARGIN

21 The irradiance of a point source is measured at a particular distance from the source and found to be $54\,W\,m^{-2}$.

1 — Particles and waves 4

What value would be measured at three times the distance from the source?

A $54\,W\,m^{-2}$

B $18\,W\,m^{-2}$

C $12\,W\,m^{-2}$

D $6{\cdot}0\,W\,m^{-2}$

E $4{\cdot}5\,W\,m^{-2}$

22 The peak voltage of a source is measured to be $10{\cdot}0\,V$.

1 — Electricity 1

What is the r.m.s. voltage value for this source?

A $14{\cdot}1\,V$

B $10{\cdot}0\,V$

C $7{\cdot}07\,V$

D $5{\cdot}0\,V$

E $2{\cdot}23\,V$

23 A $2000\,\mu F$ capacitor is completely charged when the voltage across the plates is $4{\cdot}5\,V$.

1 — Electricity 4

How much energy is stored in the capacitor when it is fully charged?

A $4{\cdot}05 \times 10^{-2}\,J$

B $2{\cdot}03 \times 10^{-2}\,J$

C $1{\cdot}01 \times 10^{-2}\,J$

D $9{\cdot}00 \times 10^{-3}\,J$

E $4{\cdot}50 \times 10^{-3}\,J$

24 Which of the following correctly describes the conduction and valence bands of an insulator?

1 — Electricity 5

A The conduction band overlaps the valence band.

B The conduction band is very close to the valence band.

C The conduction band is very far from the valence band.

D The conduction band is lower energy than the valence band.

E The conduction band is the same energy as the valence band.

25 A p–n junction is formed by joining two pieces of semiconductor.

1 — Electricity 5

In the depletion region of the junction, which of the following statements is true?

A The majority of charge carriers in the depletion region are electrons.

B The majority of charge carriers in the depletion region are holes.

C The concentration of charge carriers in the depletion region is greater than in the p or n semiconductor.

D The concentration of charge carriers in the depletion region is lower than in the p or n semiconductor.

E The concentration of charge carriers in the depletion region is the same as in the p or n semiconductor.

Paper 2

> **Total marks**: 130
>
> **Duration**: 2 hours and 15 minutes
>
> Attempt ALL questions.
>
> Reference may be made to the Data sheet on page xi and to the Relationships sheet on page xiii.
>
> Care should be taken to give an appropriate number of significant figures in the final answers to calculations.
>
> Write your answers clearly in the spaces provided in this paper. Any rough work must be written in this paper. You should score through your rough work when you have written your final copy.
>
> Use **blue** or **black** ink.

MARKS **STUDENT MARGIN**

1 Hillend is Europe's longest dry ski run with an overall piste length of 400 m, total vertical drop of 110 m and average slope angle of 16°.

A skier of total mass 70 kg ascends the slope using the ski-tow and then completes a run down the slope.

a) The velocity–time graph of the first part of the uphill ski-tow journey is shown.

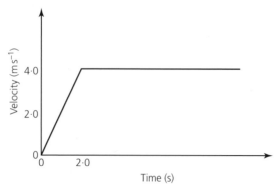

		MARKS	STUDENT MARGIN

(i) Calculate the resultant force experienced by the skier during the first 2 seconds of the ascent.

Space for working and answer

3 — Our dynamic Universe 1

(ii) Determine the resultant force experienced by the skier after the first 2 seconds of the ascent.

Space for working and answer

1 — Our dynamic Universe 1

b) Calculate the maximum kinetic energy of the skier as they arrive at the bottom of the slope.

Space for working and answer

3 — Our dynamic Universe 1

c) The actual velocity of the skier at the bottom of the slope is determined to be $20 \cdot 0 \, \mathrm{m\,s^{-1}}$.

Calculate the average frictional force over the 400 m descent.

Space for working and answer

3 — Our dynamic Universe 1

(10)

2 A car, mass 1500 kg, is towing a caravan of mass 1000 kg. The car accelerates uniformly from rest to a velocity of $22 \cdot 0 \, \mathrm{m\,s^{-1}}$ in $12 \cdot 0$ seconds.

a) Show that the acceleration of the car and caravan is $1 \cdot 83 \, \mathrm{m\,s^{-2}}$.

Space for working and answer

2 — Our dynamic Universe 1

b) Calculate the magnitude of the accelerating force provided by the car engine.

Space for working and answer

3 — Our dynamic Universe 2

c) Calculate the magnitude of the tension force in the tow bar connecting the car and caravan.

Space for working and answer

3 — Our dynamic Universe 2

(8)

3   A student is investigating the physics of snooker. Using light gates and a computer they determine the velocity of the white cue ball and the yellow ball that it hits. On a particular shot, the white hits the yellow and they both move off in the same direction along the same line as the original path of the white ball.

The student's results are shown below.

Mass of white ball: 0·17 kg

Mass of yellow ball: 0·16 kg

	Velocity before strike (m s^{-1})	Velocity after strike (m s^{-1})
white ball	3·80	0·51
yellow ball	0·00	3·49

a)   Show that momentum is conserved in the collision between the white and yellow balls.

Space for working and answer

3

Our dynamic Universe 3

b)   State whether the collision is elastic or inelastic.
You must justify your answer.

Space for working and answer

3

Our dynamic Universe 3

c)   The student now adjusts the experiment to measure the contact time between the cue and the white ball. The ball speed after being struck is 4·15 m s^{-1}. The contact time is measured as 0·35 ms.

Calculate the average force applied by the cue to the ball as it is struck.

Space for working and answer

3

Our dynamic Universe 3

(9)

MARKS   STUDENT MARGIN

4 Satellite navigation systems involve a network of satellites orbiting the Earth. Typical orbit altitudes are 20 200 km with an orbit period of 12 hours. The radius of the Earth is 6371 km and its mass is 5.97×10^{24} kg.

(9)

a) Calculate the magnitude of the velocity of a satellite in this network.
Space for working and answer

4   Our dynamic Universe 4

b) Calculate the magnitude of the gravitational force acting on a satellite of mass 250 kg in this network.
Space for working and answer

4   Our dynamic Universe 4

c) Explain why the magnitude of the satellite velocity is constant despite the unbalanced gravitational force acting on the satellite.
Space for working and answer

1   Our dynamic Universe 4

(9)

5 Muons are fundamental particles which are a constituent part of the solar radiation incident on the Earth. These muons travel at around 98% of the speed of light (0·98c).

For a stationary observer on Earth, calculate how many seconds pass on their clock for each second experienced by the muon.

Space for working and answer

3

Our dynamic Universe 5

(3)

6 Students observe an ambulance as it drives towards and then past them on the street. The ambulance is travelling at 28·0 m s⁻¹ and emits a siren with a highest tone of 440 Hz and lowest tone of 420 Hz. The speed of sound in air is 340 m s⁻¹.

a) Calculate the lowest frequency note heard by the students as the ambulance approaches.

Space for working and answer

3

Our dynamic Universe 6

b) As the ambulance passes by, the students note that the siren appears to change in frequency.

State how the frequency observed by the students changes.

1

Our dynamic Universe 6

c) Calculate the highest frequency note heard by the students as the ambulance moves away.

Space for working and answer

3

Our dynamic Universe 6

(7)

7 How many up quarks are there in an alpha particle? Justify your answer.

3

Particles and waves 2

(3)

MARKS | STUDENT MARGIN

8 A student is using electron beam apparatus to investigate the relationship between acceleration voltage and beam deflection distance. Assume the grid is marked in cm.

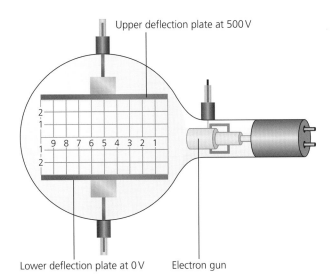

Upper deflection plate at 500 V

2
1
9 8 7 6 5 4 3 2 1
1
2

Lower deflection plate at 0 V   Electron gun

a) Sketch the electric field pattern between the two deflection plates shown below.

——————————— +500 V

——————————— 0 V

2 | Particles and waves 1

b) The student sets the acceleration voltage to be 1·25 kV.

(i) Show that the work done on each electron, as it is accelerated by the electron gun, is $2·00 \times 10^{-16}$ J.

Space for working and answer

2 | Particles and waves 1

(ii) Calculate the minimum velocity of the electrons as they exit the electron gun.

Space for working and answer

3 | Particles and waves 1

(iii) Calculate the time taken for an electron to travel through the field between the deflection plates.

Space for working and answer

3 | Particles and waves 1

(10)

9 A student states, 'There is never any charge stored in a capacitor, the total charge is always the same before and after it has been charged.'

Use your knowledge of physics to comment on this statement.

(3)

10 The following equation shows a nuclear reaction.

$$^{235}_{92}U + ^{1}_{0}n \rightarrow ^{93}_{37}Rb + ^{141}_{55}Cs + 2^{1}_{0}n$$

Particle	Mass (kg)
^{235}U	$390{\cdot}173 \times 10^{-27}$
^{93}Rb	$154{\cdot}248 \times 10^{-27}$
^{141}Cs	$233{\cdot}927 \times 10^{-27}$
^{1}n	$1{\cdot}675 \times 10^{-27}$

a) State what type of nuclear reaction is shown.

b) Explain why this type of reaction releases energy.

c) Calculate the amount of energy released by the reaction, using the data in the table.

Space for working and answer

d) A 30 MW nuclear power station is designed to use this reaction to generate electricity.

Calculate the minimum number of reactions per second required to meet this demand.

Space for working and answer

(11)

	MARKS	STUDENT MARGIN

11 The graph shows the emitted electron kinetic energy versus incident light frequency results for a series of photoelectric effect experiments using three different metals (A, B and C).

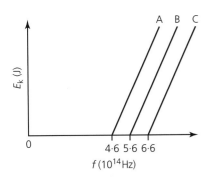

a) Explain why the graph for each metal intersects the frequency axis at a different point.

2   Particles and waves 5

b) Explain why the graph for each metal has the same gradient.

2   Particles and waves 5

c) Calculate the wavelength of the minimum frequency of light which causes electrons to be emitted from metal A.

Space for working and answer

4   Particles and waves 5

d) Estimate the colour of light associated with the minimum frequency of light which causes electrons to be emitted from metal A.

1   Particles and waves 5

(9)

MARKS STUDENT MARGIN

12 The experiment below shows the interference pattern produced when a 1 mW green laser light, 550 nm, is incident on a diffraction grating with 300 lines per mm.

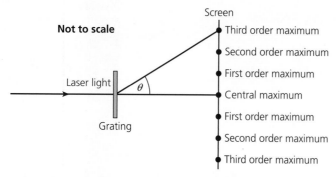

Screen

Not to scale

Laser light

θ

Grating

Third order maximum
Second order maximum
First order maximum
Central maximum
First order maximum
Second order maximum
Third order maximum

a) Explain why this experiment produces a series of equally spaced, bright green spots separated by dark regions on the screen.

3   Particles and waves 6

b) Calculate the distance from the central maximum to the second maximum observed on a screen 2·0 m from the grating.

Space for working and answer

4   Particles and waves 6

c) The green laser is now replaced with a red laser source of the same power. Describe what changes would be observed to the pattern viewed on the screen.

You must explain your answer.

3   Particles and waves 6

(10)

MARKS | STUDENT MARGIN

13 A student is investigating the relationship between incident and refracted angles for light rays passing into air from a glass block using the apparatus below.

An extract from their notebook is shown in the table.

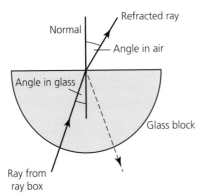

Angle in glass (°)	3·5	7·0	10·5	13·9	17·3
Angle in air (°)	5·0	10·0	15·0	20·0	25·0

a) Using all of the data, determine the refractive index of the glass block.

5 | Particles and waves 8

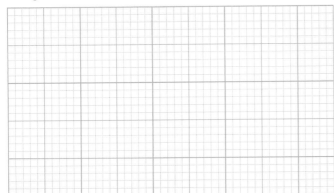

b) The student continues with the experiment and notes that for incident angles larger than a particular value, the critical angle, no light escapes the block.

(i) State what is meant by the critical angle.

1 | Particles and waves 8

(ii) Calculate the value of the critical angle for the glass block.

Space for working and answer

3 | Particles and waves 8

(9)

61

14 The diagram shows a model of part of the atomic electron energy levels for a particular element.

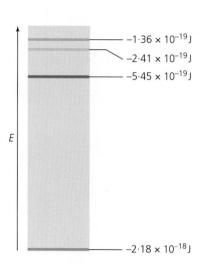

E

— $-1{\cdot}36 \times 10^{-19}$ J
— $-2{\cdot}41 \times 10^{-19}$ J
— $-5{\cdot}45 \times 10^{-19}$ J

— $-2{\cdot}18 \times 10^{-18}$ J

a) State how many electron energy level transitions are possible for this model.

1   Particles and waves 7

b) Calculate the largest wavelength of light emitted by electrons in this model.
Space for working and answer

4   Particles and waves 7

(5)

15 The diagram shows an oscilloscope trace for an AC electrical source.
The time-base is set at 4·0 ms/div and the Y-gain is set at 50 V/div.

1 div

1 div

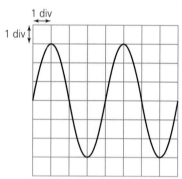

a) Calculate the frequency of this source.
Space for working and answer

4   Electricity 1

b) Calculate the voltage rating for this source.
Space for working and answer

4   Electricity 1

(8)

MARKS | STUDENT MARGIN

16 A student states, 'If it were not for the conservation of energy, we would not know about the neutrino.'

Use your knowledge of physics to comment on this statement.

3   Electricity 4

(3)

17 This circuit is used to measure the relationship between terminal potential difference and current in the load resistor, in order to determine the e.m.f. and internal resistance of the battery.

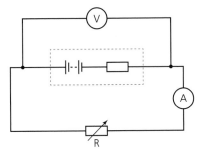

a) Explain what is meant by the terms terminal potential difference and e.m.f.

2   Electricity 3

b) The graph of the relationship between terminal potential difference and current obtained is shown below.

Use the graph to determine the e.m.f. of the supply.

1   Electricity 3

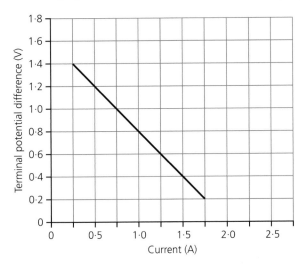

		MARKS	STUDENT MARGIN

c) Use the graph to determine the internal resistance of the supply.
Space for working and answer

MARKS: 4 — STUDENT MARGIN: Electricity 3

(7)

18 The charge on a capacitor is measured using a coulomb meter.
The results are 1·03 nC, 1·04 nC, 1·01 nC, 1·06 nC, 1·08 nC.

a) Calculate the mean value of the charge stored on the capacitor.
Space for working and answer

MARKS: 3 — STUDENT MARGIN: Electricity 4

b) Calculate the random uncertainty in the mean value of the charge stored.
Space for working and answer

MARKS: 3 — STUDENT MARGIN: Electricity 4

(6)

[130]

[END OF PRACTICE EXAM A]

Duration: 3 hours
Total marks: 155

PAPER 1 – 25 marks
Attempt ALL questions.

PAPER 2 – 130 marks
Attempt ALL questions.
Reference may be made to the Relationships sheet on page xi and to the Data sheet on page xiii.
Care should be taken to give an appropriate number of significant figures in the final answers to calculations.
Write your answers clearly in the spaces provided in this paper. Any rough work must be written in this paper. You should score through your rough work when you have written your final copy.
Use **blue** or **black** ink.

Paper 1

Total marks: 25
Duration: 45 minutes
Attempt ALL questions.

		MARKS	STUDENT MARGIN

1 The graph shows how the velocity of a car varies with time.

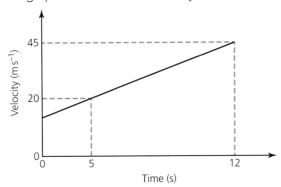

The acceleration of the car is

A $2 \cdot 9 \, \text{m s}^{-2}$

B $3 \cdot 6 \, \text{m s}^{-2}$

C $3 \cdot 8 \, \text{m s}^{-2}$

D $4 \cdot 0 \, \text{m s}^{-2}$

E $6 \cdot 4 \, \text{m s}^{-2}$.

MARKS: 1 — *Our dynamic Universe 1*

2 A mass of $10 \cdot 0 \, \text{kg}$ is hanging from a newton balance in a stationary lift. The lift then moves upwards with a constant acceleration of $0 \cdot 25 \, \text{m s}^{-2}$.

The reading on the balance is

A $9 \cdot 8 \, \text{N}$

B $10 \, \text{N}$

C $95 \cdot 5 \, \text{N}$

D $98 \, \text{N}$

E $100 \, \text{N}$.

MARKS: 1 — *Our dynamic Universe 2*

	MARKS	STUDENT MARGIN

3 A vehicle of mass 0·25 kg is moving to the right on a horizontal track at 4·5 m s⁻¹. A similar vehicle of mass 0·75 kg is moving to the left on the same track at 1·5 m s⁻¹.

The vehicles then collide and stick together.

Which of the following quantities is/are conserved in this collision?

I   the total momentum

II   the kinetic energy

III   the total energy

A   I only

B   II only

C   I and II only

D   I and III only

E   II and III only

MARKS: 1

STUDENT MARGIN: Our dynamic Universe 3

4 A golfer hits a golf ball off a fairway at an angle of 50·0° to the horizontal.

The golf ball has an initial velocity of 10·0 m s⁻¹.

What is the ball's maximum height?

A   2·1 m

B   3·0 m

C   4·0 m

D   5·1 m

E   6·5 m

MARKS: 1

STUDENT MARGIN: Our dynamic Universe 1

5 A plane lifts off from an airport at a constant acceleration from an initial speed of 85 m s⁻¹. It reaches cruising speed after 20 minutes, at which point the plane's speed is 185 m s⁻¹. It then flies at this constant speed for 30 minutes. The plane then starts descending at a constant deceleration and touches down at a speed of 105 m s⁻¹ another 30 minutes later.

Which of the following acceleration–time graphs best represents the plane's journey?

MARKS: 1

STUDENT MARGIN: Our dynamic Universe 1

A   Acceleration (m s⁻²)   Time (s)

B   Acceleration (m s⁻²)   Time (s)

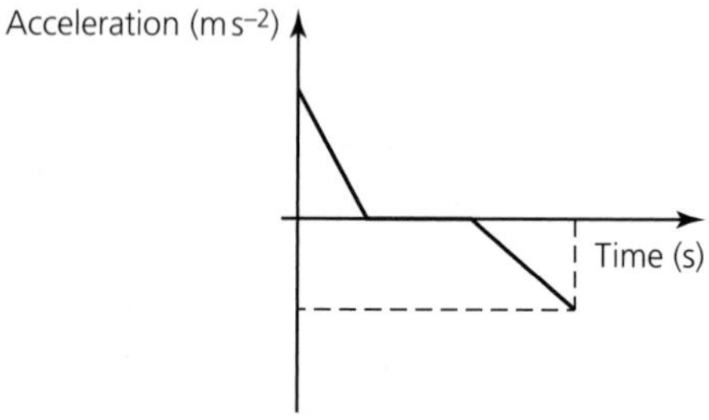

C   Acceleration (m s⁻²)   Time (s)

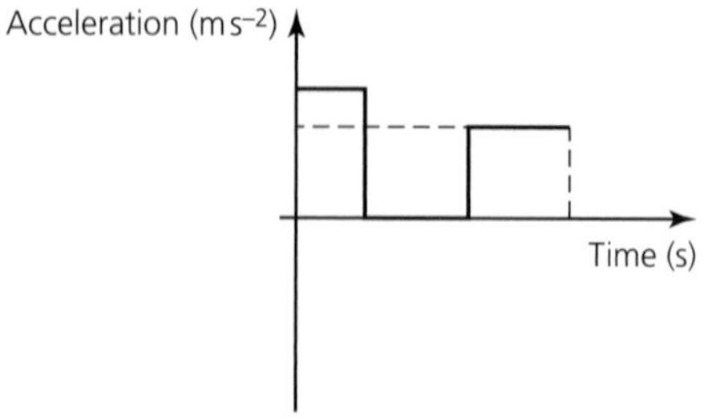

D   Acceleration (m s⁻²)   Time (s)

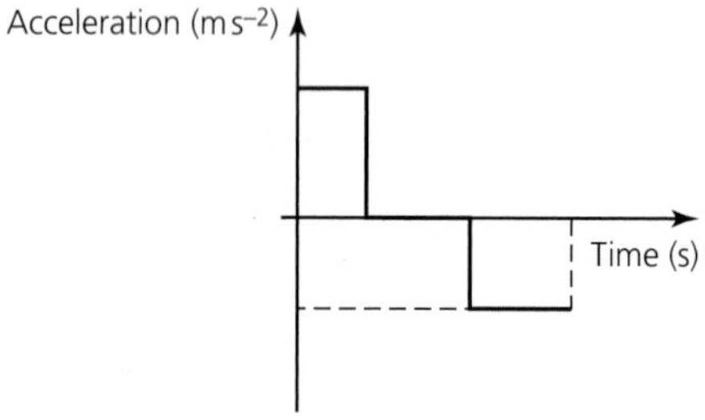

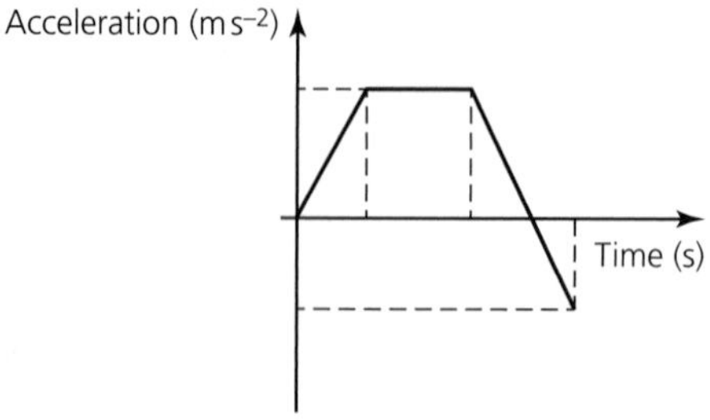

E   Acceleration (m s⁻²)   Time (s)

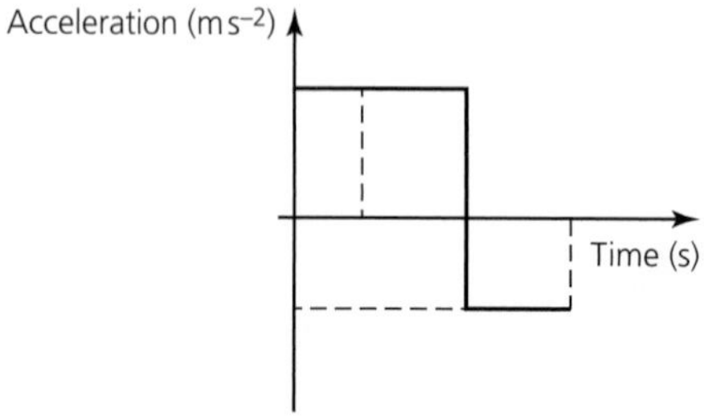

MARKS   STUDENT MARGIN

6 A snowboarder starts from rest at the top of a slope. The total mass of the snowboarder and board is 75 kg. The snowboarder travels down the slope to X through a height of 15 m.

1   Our dynamic Universe 2

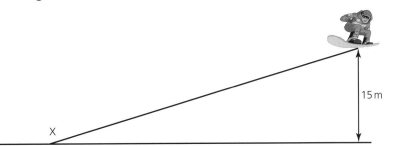

15 m

X

What is the maximum possible speed of the snowboarder at the bottom of the slope?

A   15 m s^{-1}

B   17 m s^{-1}

C   29 m s^{-1}

D   290 m s^{-1}

E   310 m s^{-1}

7 An upwards force of 55 N acts on a hot air balloon of mass 5·0 kg. The balloon starts at rest and begins to move upwards.

The velocity of the balloon after 4·0 seconds is

1   Our dynamic Universe 2

A   1·2 m s^{-1}

B   4·8 m s^{-1}

C   5·5 m s^{-1}

D   6·0 m s^{-1}

E   9·0 m s^{-1}.

8 A student makes the following statements about gravitational fields.

1   Our dynamic Universe 4

I   The closer together two objects are, the greater the gravitational attraction.

II   The magnitude of the attraction is proportional to the sum of the two masses and inversely proportional to the product of the distance between them.

III   Gravitational attraction only exists between large objects.

Which of these statements is/are correct?

A   I only

B   II only

C   I and II only

D   II and III only

E   I, II and III

9 Two 3·0 g ball bearings are held at a distance apart such that they exert a gravitational pull of $6·0 \times 10^{-14}$ N on each other.

1   Our dynamic Universe 4

How far apart are the ball bearings?

A $9·0 \times 10^{-3}$ m

B $2·0 \times 10^{-3}$ m

C $1·0 \times 10^{-2}$ m

D $1·0 \times 10^{-1}$ m

E $5·0 \times 10^{-1}$ m

	MARKS	STUDENT MARGIN

10 A spacecraft is travelling at a constant speed of 0·50c relative to the Earth. An observer on Earth measures the length of the moving spacecraft to be 200 m.

The length of the spacecraft as measured by an astronaut on the spacecraft is

A   100 m

B   200 m

C   230 m

D   300 m

E   400 m.

MARKS: 1

STUDENT MARGIN: Our dynamic Universe 5

11 A fire engine travels at a constant speed of 30 m s^{-1} as it approaches and then passes a stationary observer. The siren emits a constant frequency of 1000 Hz and the speed of sound in air is 340 m s^{-1}.

The observer hears the frequency of the siren

A   remain constant at 1000 Hz

B   continuously rise from 1000 Hz

C   continuously fall from 1000 Hz

D   as less than 1000 Hz and increase to greater than 1000 Hz as it passes

E   as greater than 1000 Hz and fall to less than 1000 Hz as it passes.

MARKS: 1

STUDENT MARGIN: Our dynamic Universe 6

12 An electron is accelerated between two plates by a potential difference of 400 V.

What is the maximum velocity of the electron after being accelerated in this field?

A $1·2 \times 10^7$ m s^{-1}

B $5·1 \times 10^7$ m s^{-1}

C $5·5 \times 10^7$ m s^{-1}

D $6·0 \times 10^7$ m s^{-1}

E $9·1 \times 10^7$ m s^{-1}

MARKS: 1

STUDENT MARGIN: Particles and waves 1

13 The statements below relate to charges in electric fields.

I   An electric charge will experience a force in an electric field.

II   An electric field applied to a conductor causes free electric charges in the conductor to move.

III When a charge moves in an electric field work is done.

Which of the statements is/are correct?

A   I only

B   II only

C   III only

D   I and III only

E   I, II and III

MARKS: 1

STUDENT MARGIN: Particles and waves 1

14 The detection of the cosmic microwave background radiation provides evidence in support of

A   the atomic structure of materials

B   wave–particle duality

C   the expansion of the Universe

D   the inverse square law

E   black holes.

MARKS: 1

STUDENT MARGIN: Our dynamic Universe 6

	MARKS	STUDENT MARGIN

15 An electron is a

    A   boson

    B   lepton

    C   meson

    D   baryon

    E   hadron.

Marks: 1 — Particles and waves 2

16 There are two main groups of fundamental particles in the Standard Model of elementary particles: fermions and bosons.

What force-mediating particles make up the family of bosons?

    A   gluon, muon, photon, graviton, W

    B   gluon, photon, Z, W, graviton

    C   gluon, photon, electron, Z, W, tau

    D   graviton, Z, muon, electron, bottom

    E   up, down, top, bottom, graviton

Marks: 1 — Particles and waves 2

17 The irradiance on a surface 0·80 m from a point source of light is I.

The irradiance on a surface 1·5 m from this source is

    A   0·12I

    B   0·28I

    C   1·2I

    D   1·4I

    E   3·5I.

Marks: 1 — Particles and waves 4

18 Two coherent light sources of wavelength $\lambda = 550$ nm, separated by a distance $d = 0·01$ mm, create the interference pattern shown in the diagram.

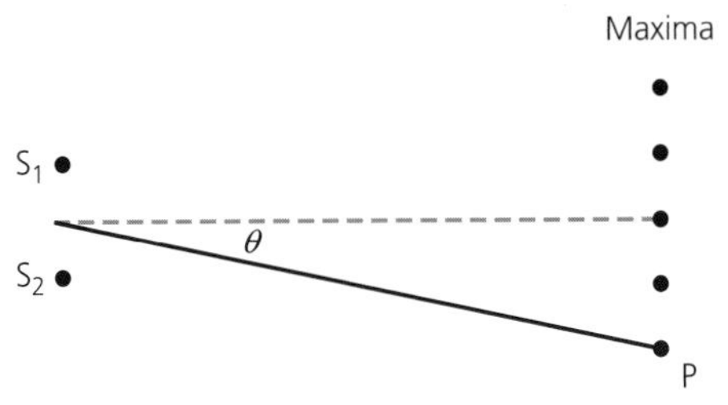

The angular location (θ) of the second bright patch P on the screen is

    A   0·57°

    B   3·4°

    C   6·3°

    D   13°

    E   25°.

Marks: 1 — Particles and waves 6

19 Red light is used to investigate the critical angle of two materials, X and Y. The path of the ray of red light is shown.

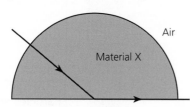 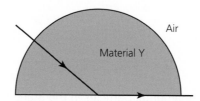

A student makes the following statements.

I   Material X has a lower refractive index than material Y.

II   The wavelength of the red light is shorter inside material X than inside material Y.

III   The red light travels at the same speed inside materials X and Y.

Which of these statements is/are correct?

A   I only

B   II only

C   III only

D   I and II only

E   I, II and III

1

Particles and waves 8

20 A circuit containing a capacitor is set up as shown.

Assume the supply has negligible internal resistance.

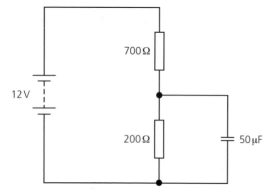

The maximum energy stored in the capacitor is

A $2 \cdot 2 \times 10^{-3}$ J

B $2 \cdot 3 \times 10^{-3}$ J

C $3 \cdot 6 \times 10^{-3}$ J

D $1 \cdot 8 \times 10^{-4}$ J

E $6 \cdot 7 \times 10^{-5}$ J.

1

Electricity 4

MARKS   STUDENT MARGIN

21 A circuit is set up as shown.

$R_1 = 24\,\Omega$, $R_2 = 18\,\Omega$ and $R_3 = 9\,\Omega$.

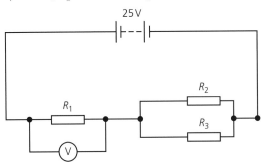

What is the reading on the voltmeter?

A   1 V

B   5 V

C   13 V

D   20 V

E   25 V

1   Electricity 2

22 The power dissipated in a resistor is 5·2 W at a current of 0·4 A.

The resistance of the resistor is

A   0·8 Ω

B   2·1 Ω

C   13 Ω

D   33 Ω

E   68 Ω.

1   Electricity 2

23 A capacitor is connected to a 12 V DC supply. The maximum energy stored in the capacitor is $1\cdot44 \times 10^{-3}$ J.

The value for the capacitance is

A   20 μF

B   120 μF

C   0·24 mF

D   17 mF

E   103 mF.

1   Electricity 4

24 A student makes the following statements about semiconductors.

I   Semiconductors have overlapping conduction and valence bands.

II   An increase in temperature increases the conductivity of a semiconductor.

III   Doping a semiconductor will decrease its conductivity.

Which of these statements is/are correct?

A   I only

B   II only

C   III only

D   I and II only

E   I, II and III

1   Electricity 5

25 An atomic weapons test yielded an explosion which was equivalent to 12·4 kilotons of TNT. This equates to $1·4 \times 10^{14}$ J.

What mass was converted into energy in this explosion?

A $1·4 \times 10^{-10}$ kg

B $1·4 \times 10^{-3}$ kg

C $1·6 \times 10^{-3}$ kg

D $1·0 \times 10^{7}$ kg

E $1·1 \times 10^{10}$ kg

Paper 2

Total marks: 130
Duration: 2 hours and 15 minutes
Attempt ALL questions.
Reference may be made to the Relationships sheet on page xi and to the Data sheet on page xiii.
Care should be taken to give an appropriate number of significant figures in the final answers to calculations.
Write your answers clearly in the spaces provided in this paper. Any rough work must be written in this paper.
You should score through your rough work when you have written your final copy.
Use **blue** or **black** ink.

MARKS | STUDENT MARGIN

1 A 1·60 kg mass is propelled along a horizontal surface as shown.
It has an initial velocity of 4·60 m s^{-1} and there is a constant frictional force of 3·20 N acting on the mass.

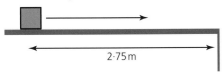

2·75 m

a) Calculate the acceleration of the mass.
Space for working and answer

3 | Our dynamic Universe 1

b) Its velocity as it reaches the edge of the surface is 3·19 m s^{-1}.
The mass falls off the end of the surface and strikes a wall of a nearby structure as shown. Losses due to air friction are negligible.
The gap between the structures is 2·25 m.

(i) Calculate how long the mass is in the air before it strikes the other structure.
Space for working and answer

2 | Our dynamic Universe 1

(ii) How far from the top of the surface does the mass strike the other wall?
Space for working and answer

3 | Our dynamic Universe 1

		MARKS	STUDENT MARGIN

(iii) What is the vertical velocity of the mass when it makes contact with the wall?

Space for working and answer

2 — Our dynamic Universe 1

(iv) Determine the magnitude of the resultant velocity when the mass makes contact with the wall.

Space for working and answer

3 — Our dynamic Universe 1

(v) The mass strikes the wall and rebounds from the wall.
Sketch the horizontal velocity–time graph for the mass from the moment it falls off the surface until 1 second after the rebound.

3 — Our dynamic Universe 1

(16)

2 The Falcon Heavy rocket is used to transport heavy loads into space. It can transport satellites into LEO (low Earth orbit) and GTO (geostationary transfer orbit) and beyond.

At launch:

Mass of rocket = $1 \cdot 47 \times 10^6$ kg

Thrust from engines = $22 \cdot 8 \times 10^6$ N

a) Calculate the weight of the rocket.

Space for working and answer

2 — Our dynamic Universe 2

b) Calculate the initial acceleration.

Space for working and answer

3 — Our dynamic Universe 2

c) The rocket places a 18 500 kg satellite in geostationary orbit at a height of 35 600 km above the Earth's surface.

Calculate the gravitational attraction between the satellite and Earth at this distance. (The diameter of the Earth at the equator is 12 700 km and the mass of the Earth is $5 \cdot 97 \times 10^{24}$ kg.)

Space for working and answer

4 — Our dynamic Universe 4

(9)

	MARKS	STUDENT MARGIN

3 As part of a training regime, an athlete runs at constant speed along a straight track with a harness attached to weights which are dragged across the ground.

The cable makes an angle of 28° to the horizontal and the frictional force between the masses and the ground is 325 N.

a) Calculate the tension in the cable.

Space for working and answer

3 — Our dynamic Universe 2

b) Calculate the work done by the athlete in moving the masses 125 m across the ground.

Space for working and answer

2 — Our dynamic Universe 2

c) The athlete repeats the exercise but on this occasion uses a shorter cable.
What difference would this make to the force exerted by the athlete?
You must justify your answer.

2 — Our dynamic Universe 2

(7)

4 A gardener has to erect a fence. A series of vertical posts are inserted into the ground and the fence is constructed around these.

The gardener uses a fence driver to insert the poles into the ground. The driver has a mass of 13 kg and is raised and dropped onto the post to hammer it in.

The post is 2·10 m high and has a mass of 4·5 kg.

The driver is raised 0·45 m above the post and dropped onto the top of the post.

a) Calculate the momentum of the driver just before it strikes the post.

Space for working and answer

3 — Our dynamic Universe 3

b) Calculate the velocity of the post and driver just after impact.

Space for working and answer

2 — Our dynamic Universe 3

		MARKS	STUDENT MARGIN

c) Each impact drives the post into the ground a small amount.

The first impact drives the post 5·5 cm into the ground.

The kinetic energy of the post and driver after impact is 42·35 J. Show that the average frictional force acting on the post is 770 N.

(You may ignore any change in gravitational potential energy of the post and driver.)

Space for working and answer

2 — Our dynamic Universe 3

d) When falling onto the post, the driver is in contact with the post for 0·35 s. Determine the force acting on the post during this impact.

Space for working and answer

3 — Our dynamic Universe 3

e) The gardener notices that each drop of the driver causes the post to go into the ground by a smaller distance.

Explain why this would be the case.

2 — Our dynamic Universe 3

(12)

5 In an attempt to explain the mechanisms by which solar flares eject particles, a physicist considered a proton travelling at 0·8c heading towards Earth.

(Distance from Sun to Earth is $1·50 \times 10^{11}$ m.)

a) Calculate the time taken by the proton to travel from the surface of the Sun to the Earth.

Space for working and answer

2 — Our dynamic Universe 5

b) Calculate the time experienced by the proton during this journey.

Space for working and answer

3 — Our dynamic Universe 5

(5)

6 Observed light from a distant galaxy contains lines from hydrogen spectra. One wavelength emitted has a value of 656 nm. The distant galaxy is travelling away at a relative velocity of $7·25 \times 10^6$ m s^{-1}.

a) Calculate the Doppler shift for this galaxy.

Space for working and answer

2 — Our dynamic Universe 6

	MARKS	STUDENT MARGIN

b) Calculate the wavelength of this spectral line when observed from Earth.

Space for working and answer

4 — Our dynamic Universe 6

c) Calculate the approximate distance, in light years, to this galaxy.

Space for working and answer

4 — Our dynamic Universe 6

(10)

7 Protons are accelerated in a cyclotron across the gap PQ as shown. The potential difference across the gap is 22 500 V.

a) How much energy could the proton gain when it passes between the gap three times?

Space for working and answer

3 — Our dynamic Universe 6

b) Explain why an alternating supply is used between P and Q.

2 — Our dynamic Universe 6

c) Describe what is happening to the protons when they are travelling within the 'D's.

2 — Our dynamic Universe 6

(7)

8 Bonnybridge has been described as the UFO capital of Scotland, if not the world, with over 300 'sightings' in one year alone.

Using your knowledge of physics, discuss the likelihood of these 'sightings' being of extraterrestrial origin.

3 — Our dynamic Universe 6

(3)

| | MARKS | STUDENT MARGIN |

9 The diagram shows the family of fundamental particles.

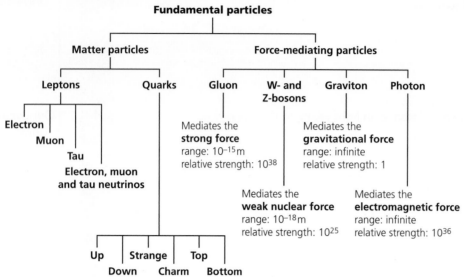

Fundamental particles

a) The gluon is the force-mediating particle for the strong force. The relative strength of the strong force is 10^{38}. It is 13 orders of magnitude stronger than the weak nuclear force.

What is the relative strength of the weak nuclear force?

1 — Particles and waves 2

b) Which force-mediating particle(s) is/are associated with the weak nuclear force?

1 — Particles and waves 2

c) State which quarks combine to form the following. Justify your answers.
(i) a proton

4 — Particles and waves 2

(ii) a neutron

(6)

10 a) Using the following data, determine a value for the binding energy **per nucleon** for the uranium nucleus $^{235}_{92}$U.

Mass of $^{235}_{92}$ U nucleus : $390 \cdot 206 \times 10^{-27}$ kg

Mass of proton: $1 \cdot 672\,62 \times 10^{-27}$ kg

Mass of neutron: $1 \cdot 674\,29 \times 10^{-27}$ kg

Space for working and answer

6 — Particles and waves 3

	MARKS	STUDENT MARGIN

b) The binding energy per nucleon of deuterium is $2 \cdot 145 \times 10^{-13}$ J. This is considerably less than that of uranium.

Explain the significance of this difference for the optimum way of generating nuclear energy.

2 — Particles and waves 3

(8)

11 A student undertakes an experiment with a light meter to investigate how the irradiance from a small lamp varies with distance. The experiment is undertaken in a darkened laboratory.

Irradiance, I $(\mathrm{W\,m^{-2}})$	Distance, d (m)
16	0·15
4·0	0·30
1·4	0·50
0·64	0·75

a) Using all this data, determine the relationship between irradiance I and the distance d from the source.

Space for working and answer

3 — Particles and waves 4

b) Explain why the experiment was conducted in a darkened room.

1 — Particles and waves 4

c) A yellow filter is placed between the lamp and the light meter.

What difference would this have on the relationship between the irradiance and the distance from the source?

You must explain your answer.

2 — Particles and waves 4

(6)

12 Ultraviolet radiation is shone onto a metal plate and electrons are released from the surface.

The frequency of the radiation is $1 \cdot 25 \times 10^{15}$ Hz.

a) Calculate the wavelength of the ultraviolet radiation.

Space for working and answer

2 — Particles and waves 5

		MARKS	STUDENT MARGIN

b) The work function of the metal is 7.95×10^{-19} J.

Calculate the maximum velocity of the electrons that are emitted from the surface.

Space for working and answer

MARKS 5 — Particles and waves 5

c) The ultraviolet source is moved closer to the metal plate.

What effect would this have on the number of electrons emitted and their velocities?

MARKS 2 — Particles and waves 5

(9)

13 The period (time for one complete swing) of a simple pendulum is given by

$$T = 2 \times \pi \times \sqrt{\frac{L}{g}} \, ,$$ where L is the length of the pendulum.

A student uses a pendulum of length 1·15 m and measures the time for one complete swing. The time is measured as 2·15 s.

Using these results, obtain a value for the acceleration due to gravity, g.

Space for working and answer

MARKS 1 — Our dynamic Universe 2

(1)

14 A newspaper carried an advertisement for an electrical heater. It claimed that it was better than any other heater of that size and rating because it was more efficient than these other heaters.

Using your knowledge of physics discuss the validity of this statement.

MARKS 3 — Electricity 3

(3)

MARKS   STUDENT MARGIN

15 A triangular wedge has been cut out of a rectangular block of glass. The triangular wedge is in the shape of an equilateral triangle so each angle is 60°. The glass has a refractive index of 1·55.

A ray of light enters the glass block and makes an angle of 22° with the normal to the triangular wedge as shown.

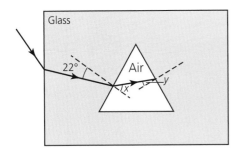

a) Calculate the angle x.   3   Particles and
    Space for working and answer   waves 8

b) Calculate the angle y.   3   Particles and
    Space for working and answer   waves 8

                                                                                  (6)

16 A student sets up a circuit as shown. The supply has an e.m.f. 12·0V and internal resistance of 1·50Ω.

The resistors connected in parallel have values 30·0Ω and 20·0Ω.

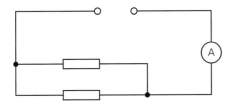

a) Calculate:
    (i)   the reading on the ammeter;   3   Electricity 3
          Space for working and answer

    (ii) the voltage from the supply.   2   Electricity 3
          Space for working and answer

b) A third resistor of 12·0Ω is available.

Where should this resistor be placed in order to increase the voltage from the supply?

You must explain your answer.

MARKS: 2

STUDENT MARGIN: Electricity 3

(7)

17 A student sets up a circuit as shown.

The student is investigating the charging and discharging characteristics of capacitors.

The student closes switches S1 and S2 simultaneously.

12 V (ignore internal resistance)

a) Calculate the initial current taken from the 12V supply.

Space for working and answer

MARKS: 3

STUDENT MARGIN: Electricity 3

b) How much charge is transferred from the supply?

Space for working and answer

MARKS: 3

STUDENT MARGIN: Electricity 4

c) Sketch a graph of the charging current with time for each of the capacitors.

MARKS: 2

STUDENT MARGIN: Electricity 4

MARKS STUDENT MARGIN

d) The student opens S2 and moves S3 to the down position.

  (i) Calculate the maximum current reading on the ammeter.

  Space for working and answer

3

Electricity 4

  (ii) The student closes S2 and returns S3 to the upwards position in order to charge both capacitors. S3 is then moved to the downwards position.

  Calculate the initial current from the capacitors.

  Space for working and answer

4

Electricity 4

(15)

[130]

[END OF PRACTICE EXAM B]

Practice Exam A

Paper 1

Question	Answer	Commentary with hints and tips
1	C	The area under a velocity–time graph is the displacement for that part of the journey. Initially constant velocity means displacement increases at a constant rate. The constant rate of decrease in velocity means the rate of increase in displacement is positive but decreasing.
2	E	The definition of acceleration is the rate of change of velocity. For a constant $5 \cdot 0\,\mathrm{m\,s^{-2}}$ acceleration, velocity increases at a rate of $5 \cdot 0\,\mathrm{m\,s^{-1}}$ every second.
3	E	The gradient of a velocity–time graph is the acceleration of the object. Each v–t has a constant gradient, so the value of acceleration must be a constant (horizontal line). The v–t gradient is negative.
4	D	Newton's first law means that constant or zero velocity implies balanced forces in the velocity vector direction. Constant horizontal and vertical velocity requires balanced forces in both the horizontal and vertical.
5	C	Resolving the vertical weight force vector ($W = mg$) into components parallel and perpendicular to the slope gives answer C.
6	C	Conservation of total linear momentum ($p = mv$) requires that the total momentum before and after the collision is the same. The velocity has halved so the total mass has doubled.
7	C	Using $F = G\dfrac{m_1 m_2}{r^2}$ where $m_1 = 4 \cdot 2 \times 10^{24}$, $m_2 = 1 \cdot 8 \times 10^4$ and $r = 3 \cdot 0 \times 10^7$ gives answer C. Forgetting to square r is a very common error.
8	C	Evidence supporting the existence of dark energy comes from the accelerating rate of expansion of the Universe.
9	D	Reading the graph shows that: ▸ the area under the curve (which is proportional to the total energy emitted) increases with temperature increase ▸ the peak wavelength value increases (moves right) as temperature decreases ▸ larger values of emitted energy occur for smaller values of wavelength λ. Therefore, I and II are correct.
10	E	Electron $\leq 10^{-18}$ m; proton $\leq 10^{-15}$ m; helium nucleus (two protons + two neutrons) > proton size.
11	D	From the course specification: fermions, the matter particles, consist of quarks (six types: up, down, strange, charm, top, bottom) and leptons (electron, muon and tau, together with their neutrinos).
12	E	The force-mediating particles are bosons: photons (electromagnetic force), W- and Z-bosons (weak force), and gluons (strong force).
13	B	The emitted electron has a range of kinetic energy but the nuclear decay is a quantum change and so should always have the same energy. This must mean another particle is emitted (the neutrino).
14	B	Field lines show the direction of force experienced by a unit positive test charge. Like charges repel.
15	A	The definition of the volt comes directly from $E_\mathrm{w} = QV$, so $V = \dfrac{E_\mathrm{w}}{Q}$.
16	C	The left-hand rule for positive charges in magnetic fields predicts the proton will be deflected upwards. The velocity vector direction changes but the velocity vector magnitude stays the same.

Question	Answer	Commentary with hints and tips
17	D	Hint: You need to know the basic operation of particle accelerators in terms of acceleration by electric field and deflection by magnetic fields.
18	B	Description of beta decay as the first evidence for the neutrino.
19	E	Coherent sources have a constant phase difference, i.e. the same frequency and wave speed in the medium.
20	D	Refractive index is always >1. Angles are measured between the ray and the normal.
21	D	Irradiance to distance is an inverse square relationship. Therefore, increasing the distance by a factor of 3 reduces the irradiance by a factor of 9 (3^2).
22	C	$V_{pk} = \sqrt{2}V_{rms}$ therefore $V_{rms} = \dfrac{V_{pk}}{\sqrt{2}}$
23	B	$E = \dfrac{1}{2}CV^2$; a common error is to forget to square the voltage.
24	C	Insulators do not conduct because there are no charge carriers in the conduction band and the energy gap between the valence and conduction bands is too large for the charge carriers to move into the conduction bands.
25	D	In the depletion region of the p–n junction, the concentration of free charge carriers is reduced by the combination of electrons and holes on the formation of the junction.

Paper 2

Question			Expected response		Max. mark	Commentary with hints and tips
1	a)	(i)	From the graph, $a = \dfrac{4\cdot0}{2\cdot0} = 2\cdot0$ m s^{-2} (1) $F = ma$ (1) $F = 70 \times 2 = 140$ N (1)		3	The slope of a v–t graph is the acceleration of the object. The resultant (unbalanced) force gives rise to the acceleration of the object.
		(ii)	From the graph, $a = 0$ m s^{-2}, therefore $F = 0$ N		1	The slope of a v–t graph is the acceleration of the object. A horizontal line has zero gradient.
	b)		$E_k = E_p$ $E_k = mgh$ (1) $E_k = 70 \times 9\cdot8 \times 110$ (1) $E_k = 7\cdot546 \times 10^4$ J $E_k = 7\cdot5 \times 10^4$ J (1)		3	Conservation of energy means that the maximum kinetic energy at the bottom of the slope is the total potential energy at the top of the slope. Poorest significant figure in the question is 2 s.f., so answer to 2 s.f.
	c)		$E_k = \dfrac{1}{2}mv^2$ (1) $E_k = \dfrac{1}{2} \times 70 \times 20^2$ $E_k = 1\cdot4 \times 10^4$ J (1) $E_w = Fs$ $(7\cdot5 \times 10^4 - 1\cdot4 \times 10^4) = F \times 400$ $F = 1\cdot5 \times 10^2$ N (1)		3	Some of the original potential energy is dissipated by work against friction. The difference between the maximum and actual kinetic energy gives the value of work against friction. Poorest significant figure in the question is 2 s.f., so answer to 2 s.f.
					(10)	

Question		Expected response		Max. mark	Commentary with hints and tips
2	a)	$v = u + at$ $22 \cdot 0 = 0 + a \times 12 \cdot 0$ (1) $a = \dfrac{22 \cdot 0}{12 \cdot 0}$ $a = 1 \cdot 83 \, \mathrm{m\,s^{-2}}$ (1)		2	Tip: In 'show that' questions, you must write down the equation, substitute the correct numbers for the symbols and show an equation which leads to the answer. The final line should show the value and units for the answer.
	b)	$F = ma$ (1) $F = (1500 + 1000) \times 1 \cdot 83$ (1) $F = 4575 \, \mathrm{N}$ $F = 4 \cdot 58 \times 10^{3} \, \mathrm{N}$ (1)		3	The car engine accelerates both the car and caravan, so both masses must be used. Poorest significant figure in the question is 3 s.f., so answer to 3 s.f.
	c)	$F = ma$ (1) $F = (1000) \times 1 \cdot 83$ (1) $F = 1830$ $F = 1 \cdot 83 \times 10^{3} \, \mathrm{N}$ (1)		3	The tension in the tow bar provides the acceleration force for the caravan, so just the mass of the caravan is used. Poorest significant figure in the question is 3 s.f., so answer to 3 s.f.
				(8)	
3	a)	$p_{\text{before}} = m_1 u_1 + m_2 u_2$ $p_{\text{before}} = 0 \cdot 17 \times 3 \cdot 8 + 0 \cdot 16 \times 0 \cdot 0$ (1) $p_{\text{before}} = 0 \cdot 65 \, \mathrm{kg\,m\,s^{-1}}$ $p_{\text{after}} = m_1 v_1 + m_2 v_2$ $p_{\text{after}} = 0 \cdot 17 \times 0 \cdot 51 + 0 \cdot 16 \times 3 \cdot 49$ (1) $p_{\text{after}} = 0 \cdot 65 \, \mathrm{kg\,m\,s^{-1}}$ (1)		3	Momentum conservation means that the total linear momentum before and after collision is the same. Note that this is shown to be true when using the correct number of significant figures (i.e. 2 s.f.).
	b)	Before: $E_k = \dfrac{1}{2} m v^2$ $E_k = \dfrac{1}{2} \times 0 \cdot 17 \times 3 \cdot 8^2$ $E_k = 1 \cdot 23 \, \mathrm{J}$ (1) After: $E_k = \dfrac{1}{2} m v^2$ $E_k = \dfrac{1}{2} \times 0 \cdot 17 \times 0 \cdot 51^2 + \dfrac{1}{2} \times 0 \cdot 16 \times 3 \cdot 49^2$ $E_k = 0 \cdot 997 \, \mathrm{J}$ (1) The collision is inelastic as the kinetic energy is not conserved. (1)		3	Kinetic energy conservation determines whether the collision is elastic or not.
	c)	Impulse $= F \times t = (mv - mu)$ (1) $F \times 0 \cdot 35 \times 10^{-3} = 0 \cdot 17 \times 4 \cdot 15$ (1) $F = 2 \cdot 02 \times 10^{3} \, \mathrm{N}$ $F = 2 \cdot 0 \times 10^{3} \, \mathrm{N}$ (1)		3	Impulse is given by both $F \times t$ **and** $(mv - mu)$. The cue ball starts at rest, therefore $u = 0 \cdot 0 \, \mathrm{m\,s^{-1}}$. The time in the question is in milliseconds ($\times 10^{-3}$ s). Poorest significant figure in the question is 2 s.f., so answer to 2 s.f.
				(9)	

Question		Expected response		Max. mark	Commentary with hints and tips
4	a)	$s = 2\pi r$ $s = 2\pi(20\,200 + 6371) \times 10^3$ (1) $s = vt$ (1) $v = \dfrac{2\pi(20\,200 + 6371) \times 10^3}{12 \times 60 \times 60}$ (1) $v = 3{\cdot}8646 \times 10^3\,\mathrm{m\,s^{-1}}$ $v = 3{\cdot}9 \times 10^3\,\mathrm{m\,s^{-1}}$ (1)		4	The distance travelled by the satellite is the circumference of a circular orbit. The time for the journey is the period of the orbit. The radius of orbit = the altitude + the radius of the Earth. The distances in the question are in km. Poorest significant figure in the question is 2 s.f., so answer to 2 s.f.
	b)	$r = (20\,200 + 6371) \times 10^3\,\mathrm{m}$ (1) $F = \dfrac{Gm_1 m_2}{r^2}$ (1) $F = \dfrac{6{\cdot}67 \times 10^{-11} \times 5{\cdot}97 \times 10^{24} \times 250}{(26\,571 \times 10^3)^2}$ (1) $F = 141{\cdot}0\,\mathrm{N}$ $F = 1{\cdot}41 \times 10^2\,\mathrm{N}$ (1)		4	The radius of orbit = the altitude + the radius of the Earth. The distances in the question are in km. Poorest significant figure in the question is 3 s.f., so answer to 3 s.f.
	c)	Acceleration is a change of velocity vector. The velocity vector direction is constantly changing while the magnitude is a constant value.		1	Hint: You need to be able to select the correct relationships from the Relationship sheet to solve problems involving balanced and unbalanced forces, mass and acceleration.
				(9)	
5		$t' = \dfrac{t}{\sqrt{1 - \left(\dfrac{v}{c}\right)^2}}$ (1) $t' = \dfrac{1}{\sqrt{1 - (0{\cdot}98)^2}}$ (1) $t' = 5{\cdot}02519\,\mathrm{s}$ $t' = 5{\cdot}0\,\mathrm{s}$ (1)		3	The velocity is given as $0{\cdot}98c$, therefore $\dfrac{v}{c} = 0{\cdot}98$. The question asks for the muon time for each second of stationary observer, so $t = 1\,\mathrm{s}$. Poorest significant figure in the question is 2 s.f., so answer to 2 s.f.
				(3)	
6	a)	$f_o = f_s\left(\dfrac{v}{v - v_s}\right)$ (1) $f_o = 420\left(\dfrac{340}{340 - 28{\cdot}0}\right)$ (1) $f_o = 457{\cdot}69\,\mathrm{Hz}$ $f_o = 458\,\mathrm{Hz}$ (1)		3	The ambulance is approaching (separation is reducing) so the equation has $v - v_s$ in the denominator. Poorest significant figure in the question is 3 s.f., so answer to 3 s.f.
	b)	The frequency appears to change from higher to lower as the ambulance moves past the observers.		1	The Doppler effect causes shifts in wavelengths of sound and light.
	c)	$f_o = f_s\left(\dfrac{v}{v + v_s}\right)$ (1) $f_o = 440\left(\dfrac{340}{340 + 28{\cdot}0}\right)$ (1) $f_o = 406{\cdot}52\,\mathrm{Hz}$ $f_o = 407\,\mathrm{Hz}$ (1)		3	The ambulance is moving away (separation is increasing) so the equation has $v + v_s$ in the denominator. Poorest significant figure in the question is 3 s.f., so answer to 3 s.f.
				(7)	

Question			Expected response	Max. mark	Commentary with hints and tips
7			Six up quarks (1) An alpha particle consists of two protons and two neutrons. Each proton has uud quarks and each neutron ddu quarks. (1)	3	Both protons and neutrons are baryons. They contain up (u) and down (d) quarks.
				(3)	
8	a)			2	Electric fields **by definition** show the direction of the force experienced by a positive charge, i.e. downward here. Parallel plates gives rise to a uniform electric field – equally spaced vertical lines.
	b)	(i)	$E_W = QV$ (1) $E_W = 1 \cdot 6 \times 10^{-19} \times 1 \cdot 25 \times 10^3$ $E_W = 2 \cdot 00 \times 10^{-16}\,\text{J}$ (1)	2	Tip: In 'show that' questions, you must write down the equation, substitute the correct numbers for the symbols and show an equation which leads to the answer. The final line should show the value and units for the answer.
		(ii)	By conservation of energy $E_W = E_k$ $E_k = \dfrac{1}{2}mv^2 = 2 \cdot 00 \times 10^{-16}$ (1) $\dfrac{1}{2} \times 9 \cdot 11 \times 10^{-31} \times v^2 = 2 \cdot 00 \times 10^{-16}$ (1) $v = \sqrt{\dfrac{2 \times 2 \cdot 00 \times 10^{-16}}{9 \cdot 11 \times 10^{-31}}}$ $v = 2 \cdot 095 \times 10^7\,\text{m s}^{-1}$ $v = 2 \cdot 10 \times 10^7\,\text{m s}^{-1}$ (1)	3	Conservation of energy means the work done by the field is equivalent to the kinetic energy gained by the electron. Poorest significant figure in the question is 3 s.f., so answer to 3 s.f.
		(iii)	Constant horizontal velocity $(v = 2 \cdot 1 \times 10^7\,\text{m s}^{-1})$ $s = vt$ (1) $10 \times 10^{-2} = 2 \cdot 095 \times 10^7 \times t$ (1) $t = \dfrac{10 \times 10^{-2}}{2 \cdot 095 \times 10^7}$ $t = 4 \cdot 77 \times 10^{-9}\,\text{s}$ $t = 4 \cdot 8 \times 10^{-9}\,\text{s}$ (1)	3	The field accelerated the electron vertically (not horizontally). Therefore, constant velocity equation. Poorest significant figure in the question is 2 s.f., so answer to 2 s.f.
				(10)	

Question		Expected response	Max. mark	Commentary with hints and tips
9		**Sample answer** Possible responses could include some of the following concepts/points: ▶ Charge is conserved in an electrical circuit. ▶ A capacitor is two conducting surfaces (plates) separated by an insulator. ▶ Overall a capacitor is neutral whether it is charged or not. ▶ A charged capacitor stores energy. ▶ There is a charge separation in the capacitor with negative charge accumulating on one plate and positive charge on the other. ▶ The energy in a capacitor is stored in the electric field between the two plates of the capacitor. ▶ The electrical potential energy of the supply is transferred to the electrical potential energy of the field in the capacitor. ▶ Not all the electrical potential energy of the supply is transferred to the capacitor. ▶ The work done of each coulomb passing through the supply is $E_w = QV$. ▶ The energy stored in the capacitor for each coulomb of charge on the plates is $E = \frac{1}{2}QV$.	3	This is an open-ended question: a variety of physics statements and descriptions can be used to answer this question. Marks are awarded on the basis of whether the answer overall demonstrates 'no' (0 marks), 'limited' (1 mark), 'reasonable' (2 marks) or 'good' (3 marks) understanding. This type of answer might include a statement of the principles involved, a relationship or an equation, and the application of these to respond to the problem. 3 marks would be awarded to an answer which demonstrates a good understanding of the physics involved. The answer would show a good comprehension of the physics of the situation, provided in a logically correct sequence.
			(3)	
10	a)	Induced nuclear fission	1	Hint: You need to be able to use nuclear equations to describe radioactive decay and fission (spontaneous and induced).
	b)	There is a mass difference between the reactants and products. (1) This mass is converted to energy (using $E = mc^2$). (1)	2	Hint: You need to be able to select the correct relationships from the Relationship sheet to solve problems involving the mass loss and the energy released by a nuclear reaction.
	c)	Mass before: $390 \cdot 173 + 1 \cdot 675 = 391 \cdot 848$ Mass after: $154 \cdot 248 + 233 \cdot 927 + 3 \cdot 35 = 391 \cdot 525$ Mass difference $= 391 \cdot 848 - 391 \cdot 525$ $\qquad = 0 \cdot 323 \times 10^{-27}\,\text{kg}$ (1) $E = mc^2$ (1) $E = 0 \cdot 323 \times 10^{-27} \times (3 \times 10^8)^2$ (1) $E = 2 \cdot 907 \times 10^{-11}\,\text{J}$ (1)	4	It is much easier to have all masses in the same unit (e.g. $\times 10^{-27}$ kg). Laying out the calculation as shown makes the arithmetic clear.

Question		Expected response	Max. mark	Commentary with hints and tips
	d)	$P = \dfrac{E}{t}$ $N = \dfrac{P}{E}$ (1) $N = \dfrac{30 \times 10^6}{2 \cdot 907 \times 10^{-11}}$ (1) $N = 1 \cdot 03199 \times 10^{18}$ (1) $N = 1 \cdot 0 \times 10^{18}$ (1)	4	The number of reactions per second (N) is given by $\dfrac{P}{E}$. Poorest significant figure in the question is 2 s.f., so answer to 2 s.f.
			(11)	
11	a)	The work function (minimum energy needed to remove an electron from the metal surface) is given by hf_o. (1) Work function is dependent on the metal structure and is therefore different for each metal. (1)	2	$E_k = hf_o - hf$ is the equation for photoelectric emission. Using $y = mx + c$ for any straight line gives the x-axis intercept as f_o.
	b)	The relationship between incident photon energy and frequency is $E = hf$. (1) The gradient of each energy–frequency line must therefore be the same value (i.e. Planck's constant, h). (1)	2	$E_k = hf_o - hf$ is the equation for photoelectric emission. Using $y = mx + c$ for any straight line gives the gradient as h.
	c)	From graph, minimum frequency is $4 \cdot 6 \times 10^{14}$ Hz (1) $v = f\lambda$ (1) $3 \times 10^8 = 4 \cdot 6 \times 10^{14} \times \lambda$ (1) $\lambda = 6 \cdot 5217 \times 10^{-7}$ m $\lambda = 6 \cdot 5 \times 10^{-7}$ m (1)	4	Poorest significant figure in the question is 2 s.f., so answer to 2 s.f.
	d)	650 nm light is in the red range of the visible spectrum.	1	Spectral lines listed on the Data sheet give example wavelengths and colours.
			(9)	
12	a)	Laser light is separated into multiple coherent sources by the grating. (1) Light from these coherent sources travels different distances to reach the screen. (1) When this path difference is an exact multiple of the light wavelength, the light from multiple sources interferes constructively to give a bright spot (all other path differences result in destructive interference). (1)	3	Answer must include: ▸ coherent sources ▸ path difference ▸ condition for constructive interference.

Question		Expected response	Max. mark	Commentary with hints and tips
	b)	$d = \dfrac{1 \times 10^{-3}}{300} = 3 \cdot 33 \times 10^{-6}\,\text{m}$ (1) $m\lambda = d\sin\theta = d\dfrac{D}{L}$ (1) $2 \times 550 \times 10^{-9} = 3 \cdot 33 \times 10^{-6} \times \dfrac{D}{2 \cdot 0}$ (1) $D = 0 \cdot 660\,67\,\text{m}$ $D = 0 \cdot 66\,\text{m}$ (1)	4	300 lines per millimetre gives a line spacing of $\dfrac{1\,\text{mm}}{300}$ as shown. The geometry of the layout means that $\sin\theta = \tan\theta = \dfrac{D}{L}$ where L is the large distance to the screen and D is the distance between the central maximum and the maximum being observed. Poorest significant figure in the question is 2 s.f., so answer to 2 s.f.
	c)	The wavelength of red light is larger than that of green light. (1) Given $m\lambda = d\sin\theta$, increasing λ while holding all other variables constant means that $\sin\theta$ and so θ increases, i.e. the pattern spacing increases. (1) The output power and irradiance are constant and so the brightness of the spots should remain constant. (1)	3	Hint: You need to be able to select the correct relationships from the Relationship sheet to solve problems involving grating spacing, wavelength, order number and angle to the maximum.
			(10)	
13	a)	Calculate the ratio sin (angle in air) / sin (angle in glass) for each pair of data. (table below) The constant ratio is the refractive index, i.e. $n = 1 \cdot 42$. **OR** Plot the graph of sin (angle in air) vs sin (angle in glass) and determine the gradient of the best-fit line. i.e. $n = 1 \cdot 42$.	5	When the question says 'use all the data', **either**: ▸ calculate the appropriate ratio for each pair of data ▸ explicitly state the constant ratio may be used to derive the value **OR** plot a graph with: ▸ linear scale axes ▸ labels and units on each axis ▸ accurately plotted data points ▸ a best-fit straight line and calculate the gradient of the best-fit line (not necessarily using the data points) to derive the value.

sin (angle in glass)	0·06	0·12	0·18	0·24	0·30
sin (angle in air)	0·09	0·17	0·26	0·34	0·42
sin (angle in air) / sin (angle in glass)	1·42	1·42	1·42	1·42	1·42

Question			Expected response	Max. mark	Commentary with hints and tips
	b)	(i)	The critical angle is the angle of incidence which produces an angle of refraction of 90°. **OR** The critical angle is the angle of incidence beyond which total internal reflection occurs.	1	The definition of critical angle in the course specification is: the angle of incidence which produces an angle of refraction of 90°. Total internal reflection occurs when the angle of incidence is greater than the critical angle.
		(ii)	$\sin\theta_c = \dfrac{1}{n}$ (1) $\theta_c = \sin^{-1}\left(\dfrac{1}{1\cdot42}\right)$ (1) $\theta_c = 44\cdot76°$ $\theta_c = 45°$ (1)	3	Poorest significant figure in the question is 2 s.f., so answer to 2 s.f.
				(9)	
14	a)		Six	1	There are six possible ways of moving between the atomic electron energy levels shown.
	b)		$E = E_3 - E_2 = (-1\cdot36 - -2\cdot41) \times 10^{-19}$ $E = 1\cdot05 \times 10^{-19}\,\text{J}$ (1) $E = hf$ $1\cdot05 \times 10^{-19} = 6\cdot63 \times 10^{-34} \times f$ $f = 1\cdot5988 \times 10^{14}\,\text{Hz}$ (1) $v = f\lambda$ $3 \times 10^8 = 1\cdot5988 \times 10^{14} \times \lambda$ (1) $\lambda = 1\cdot876 \times 10^{-6}\,\text{m}$ $\lambda = 1\cdot88 \times 10^{-6}\,\text{m}$ (1)	4	The largest wavelength must have the smallest frequency. The smallest frequency corresponds to the smallest energy gap between levels. You must include both correct relationships. Poorest significant figure in the question is 3 s.f., so answer to 3 s.f.
				(5)	
15	a)		Period $T = 4 \times 4\cdot0 \times 10^{-3}$ $T = 16 \times 10^{-3}\,\text{s}$ (1) $f = \dfrac{1}{T}$ (1) $f = \dfrac{1}{16 \times 10^{-3}}$ (1) $f = 62\cdot5\,\text{Hz}$ $f = 63\,\text{Hz}$ (1)	4	Count the number of squares for one complete wave and use the time-base setting to calculate the time for one wave. Poorest significant figure in the question is 2 s.f., so answer to 2 s.f.
	b)		Peak voltage $V_{pk} = 3 \times 50$ $V_{pk} = 150\,\text{V}$ (1) $V_{pk} = \sqrt{2}V_{rms}$ (1) $150 = \sqrt{2}V_{rms}$ (1) $V_{rms} = \dfrac{150}{\sqrt{2}}$ $V_{rms} = 106\cdot066$ $V_{rms} = 110\,\text{V}$ (1)	4	Count the number of squares between the mid point and the peak and use the Y-gain setting to calculate the peak voltage. Poorest significant figure in the question is 2 s.f., so answer to 2 s.f.
				(8)	

Question		Expected response	Max. mark	Commentary with hints and tips
16		**Sample answer** Possible responses could include some of the following concepts/points: ▶ Conservation of energy means that the total energy of a system is constant in the absence of work done on or by the system. ▶ Neutrinos were first proposed as an explanation of the apparent non-conservation of energy observed in beta decay. ▶ Beta decay is the emission of a fast-moving electron by the nucleus of an atom. ▶ Beta decay is a quantum change in the energy state of the nucleus emitting the beta particle, i.e. the same amount of energy is transferred ('lost') by the nucleus to the emitted particle. ▶ The beta particles emitted by atoms of the same type have a range of kinetic energies. ▶ There must be another particle emitted with a kinetic energy equal to the difference between that of the quantum change and the kinetic energy of the beta particle. ▶ This particle is uncharged, as it does not leave a track in a cloud chamber. ▶ Beta decay occurs when a neutron in the nucleus spontaneously transforms into a proton. ▶ The neutrino emitted in beta decay is antimatter.	3	This is an open-ended question: a variety of physics statements and descriptions can be used to answer this question. Marks are awarded on the basis of whether the answer overall demonstrates 'no' (0 marks), 'limited' (1 mark), 'reasonable' (2 marks) or 'good' (3 marks) understanding. This type of answer might include a statement of the principles involved, a relationship or an equation, and the application of these to respond to the problem. 3 marks would be awarded to an answer which demonstrates a good understanding of the physics involved. The answer would show a good comprehension of the physics of the situation, provided in a logically correct sequence.
			(3)	
17	a)	Terminal potential difference is the amount of energy per coulomb of charge delivered to the circuit components by an electrical source. (1) E.m.f. is the amount of energy gained by each coulomb of charge as it passes through an electrical source. (1)	2	Tip: These definitions (and any others in the course specification) should be learned as part of your revision.
	b)	1·6 V	1	The value of e.m.f. is the point at which the line intersects the voltage axis.

Question		Expected response		Max. mark	Commentary with hints and tips
	c)	Gradient $= \dfrac{(y_2 - y_1)}{(x_2 - x_1)}$	(1)	4	Internal resistance is given by the gradient of the graph.
		Gradient $= \dfrac{(1\cdot6 - 0\cdot4)}{(0 - 1\cdot5)}$	(1)		$V = -rI + E$
		Gradient $= -0\cdot80$	(1)		$y = mx + c$
		So internal resistance, $r = 0\cdot80\,\Omega$	(1)		so gradient $m = -r$
				(7)	
18	a)	Mean $= \dfrac{\text{sum}}{\text{count}}$	(1)	3	The mean of a set of repeated measurements is the best estimate of the 'true' value of the quantity being measured.
		Mean $= \dfrac{1\cdot03 + 1\cdot04 + 1\cdot01 + 1\cdot06 + 1\cdot08}{5}$	(1)		Tip: Use the appropriate number of significant figures in your final answers. This means that the final answer can have no more significant figures than the value with the least number of significant figures used in the calculation.
		Mean $= 1\cdot044$			
		Mean $= 1\cdot04\,\text{nC}$	(1)		
	b)	Random uncertainty $= \dfrac{\text{range}}{\text{number of values}}$	(1)	3	Uncertainty should only have 1 s.f.
		$= \dfrac{(1\cdot08 - 1\cdot01)}{5}$	(1)		
		$= 0\cdot014$			
		$= 0\cdot01\,\text{nC}$	(1)		
				(6)	
				[130]	

Practice Exam B

Paper 1

Question	Answer	Commentary with hints and tips
1	B	The acceleration is $\dfrac{\text{change in } v}{\text{time taken}} = \dfrac{45-20}{12-5} = 3\cdot57 = 3\cdot6\,\mathrm{m\,s^{-2}}$.
2	E	Weight plus force required to accelerate, $10 \times 9\cdot8 + 9\cdot8 \times 0\cdot25 = 100\cdot5 = 100\,\mathrm{N}$.
3	D	In a collision, momentum and total energy are conserved.
4	B	Calculate the vertical component of velocity then use equations of motion to determine the height.
5	A	It is the only graph which has a positive, zero and negative acceleration.
6	B	Use the principle of conservation of energy; $mgh = \dfrac{1}{2}\,mv^{2}$.
7	B	The unbalanced force needs to be calculated, then acceleration is used to determine velocity. Don't forget to calculate the unbalanced force $= 6\,\mathrm{N}$
8	A	Hint: You need to use knowledge of Newton's law of universal gravitation.
9	D	Use $F = G\dfrac{m_1 m_2}{r^2}$ and the value for G, rearranging for r.
10	C	Use the length contraction relationship here but rearrange to give the length of the spaceship relative to the observer on Earth.
11	E	Hint: You need to know the Doppler effect causes shifts in wavelengths of sound and light. For example, the change in frequency due to the approaching and passing of the fire engine.
12	A	Conversion of work to energy question; $QV = \dfrac{1}{2}\,mv^{2}$.
13	E	Exemplifying the effect of an electric field on an electric charge.
14	C	Hint: You need to know what evidence there is for the Big Bang theory and subsequent expansion of the Universe: cosmic microwave background radiation, the abundance of the elements hydrogen and helium, the darkness of the sky (Olbers' paradox) and the large number of galaxies showing redshift rather than blueshift.
15	B	Hint: You need to be familiar with all the fundamental particles in the Standard Model.
16	B	Hint: You need to be familiar with all the fundamental particles in the Standard Model.
17	B	Hint: You need to know that irradiance is inversely proportional to the square of the distance from a point source (inverse square law). You need to be able to use the correct relationship to solve problems involving irradiance and distance from a point source of light. $I = \dfrac{k}{d^2}$ $I_1 d_1^2 = I_2 d_2^2$
18	C	Hint: You need to be able to select and use the appropriate relationship involving grating spacing, wavelength, order number and angle to maximum. $d\sin\theta = m\lambda$

Question	Answer	Commentary with hints and tips
19	C	Light travelling through different media and relationship between refractive index and critical angle.
20	C	$E = \frac{1}{2}CV^2$; a common error is to forget to square the voltage.
21	D	Use Ohm's law and the behaviour of resistors in parallel and series.
22	D	$P = I^2 R$; significant figures apply.
23	A	$E = \frac{1}{2}CV^2$; rearrangement may cause errors.
24	B	Hint: You need to know the properties of semiconductors, and how temperature and doping with impurities affects these properties.
25	C	$E = mc^2$

Paper 2

Question			Expected response	Max. mark	Commentary with hints and tips
1	a)		$a = \dfrac{F}{m}$ (1) $= \dfrac{-3\cdot2}{1\cdot6}$ (1) $= -2\cdot0\,\mathrm{m\,s^{-2}}$ (1)	3	Unbalanced force and simple $a = \dfrac{F}{m}$. Frictional force is acting *against*, direction of movement is therefore negative.
	b)	(i)	$t = \dfrac{s}{v}$ (1) $= \dfrac{2\cdot25}{3\cdot19} = 0\cdot705\ \mathrm{s}$ (1)	2	This is a simple distance, speed, time question. Although the ball is falling, don't be confused into thinking g is involved. Horizontal velocity is not affected by g.
		(ii)	$s = ut + \dfrac{1}{2}at^2$ (1) $s = 0\cdot0 \times t + \dfrac{1}{2} \times 9\cdot8 \times 0\cdot705^2$ (1) $= 2\cdot44\,\mathrm{m}$ (1)	3	Selection of appropriate equation. This refers to vertical motion therefore g is required and initial vertical velocity is 0. This is where the vertical acceleration of the ball is key. Equations of motion with a as g need to be used. You are asked for the distance from the top s and already know t, u (zero) and a.
		(iii)	$v = u + at$ (1) $= 0 + 9\cdot8 \times 0\cdot705$ $= 6\cdot91$ $= 6\cdot9\,\mathrm{m\,s^{-1}}$ (1)	2	Simple use of equation of motion with $u = 0$.
		(iv)	Resultant velocity$^2 = v_\mathrm{h}^2 + v_\mathrm{v}^2$ (1) $= 3\cdot19^2 + 6\cdot91^2$ $= 57\cdot92$ (1) Resultant velocity $= 7\cdot611 = 7\cdot6\,\mathrm{m\,s^{-1}}$ (1)	3	Resolution of horizontal and vertical velocities. Use simple trigonometry with horizontal and vertical velocities.
		(v)		3	Ball rebounds in opposite direction, therefore velocity is negative.
				(16)	

Question		Expected response		Max. mark	Commentary with hints and tips
2	a)	$W = mg = 1.47 \times 10^6 \times 9.8$ $\qquad$ (1) $= 1.44 \times 10^7$ $= 1.4 \times 10^7\,\text{N}$ $\qquad$ (1)		2	Determination of weight from mass of rocket.
	b)	Unbalanced force $= 22.8 \times 10^6 - 1.44 \times 10^7$ $\qquad$ (1) $= 8.39 \times 10^6\,\text{N}$ $\qquad$ (1) $a = \dfrac{F}{m} = \dfrac{8.39 \times 10^6}{1.47 \times 10^6} = 5.71\,\text{m s}^{-2}$ $\qquad$ (1)		3	Need to calculate unbalanced force: thrust – weight. This is then used to calculate initial acceleration.
	c)	$r = 6350 + 35\,600 = 41\,950\,\text{km}$ $\qquad$ (1) $F = G\dfrac{m_1 m_2}{r^2}$ $\qquad$ (1) $= 6.67 \times 10^{-11} \times \dfrac{18\,500 \times 5.97 \times 10^{24}}{(4.195 \times 10^7)^2}$ $\qquad$ (1) $= 4186 = 4190\,\text{N}$ $\qquad$ (1)		4	Need to calculate distance from centre of mass. This is distance from surface to centre plus height above surface. Calculation of the distance between the masses and conversion to m and kg may cause errors in this question.
				(9)	
3	a)	$\cos 28 = \dfrac{325}{\text{tension}}$ $\qquad$ (1) $\text{tension} = \dfrac{325}{\cos 28}$ $\qquad$ (1) $= 368 = 370\,\text{N}$ $\qquad$ (1)		3	Identifying horizontal component of tension as 325 N is key. This allows the tension in rope to be calculated using trigonometry.
	b)	$E_{\text{w}} = 325 \times 125$ $\qquad$ (1) $= 40\,625 = 40\,600\,\text{J}$ $\qquad$ (1)		2	Work done is force × distance in the direction of travel, therefore you need to use the horizontal component of the tension of cable.
	c)	Shorter cable means greater angle. Greater angle means greater tension in the cable. $\qquad$ (1) This means athlete must generate greater force to move the masses. $\qquad$ (1)		2	Tip: Don't forget to say how this affects the athlete.
				(7)	
4	a)	$v = \sqrt{2 \times 9.8 \times 0.45}$ $\qquad$ (1) $= 2.97\,\text{m s}^{-1}$ $\qquad$ (1) Momentum = mass × velocity $= 13 \times 2.97 = 38.61$ $= 39\,\text{kg m s}^{-1}$ $\qquad$ (1)		3	Use equation for the velocity of a falling object to determine velocity at impact. This velocity is used in $m \times v$ to determine momentum.
	b)	Momentum before = momentum after (1) $39 = m \times v = 17.5 \times v$ $v = \dfrac{39}{17.5} = 2.22 = 2.2\,\text{m s}^{-1}$ $\qquad$ (1)		2	Conservation of momentum and straightforward application of formula.

Question		Expected response		Max. mark	Commentary with hints and tips
	c)	Work done = force × distance	(1)	2	Kinetic energy is equated to work done overcoming average frictional force. Conversion from cm to m often causes errors. In a show question the equation and final answer needs to be included for full marks to be achieved.
		$\text{Force} = \dfrac{\text{work done}}{\text{distance}} = \dfrac{42 \cdot 35}{0 \cdot 055} = 770\,\text{N}$	(1)		
	d)	$F \times t = m \times \Delta v$	(1)	3	Use impulse equation.
		$F = \dfrac{m \times \Delta v}{t} = \dfrac{13 \times 2 \cdot 97}{0 \cdot 35}$	(1)		
		$= 110 \cdot 3 = 110\,\text{N}$	(1)		
	e)	The deeper the post is in the ground, the greater frictional force there is	(1)	2	Hint: This question is worth 2 marks, so make sure you make two points in your explanation.
		due to the post being in contact with more of the Earth.	(1)		
				(12)	
5	a)	$T = \dfrac{d}{v}$	(1)	2	Tip: Take care with your scientific notation when carrying out this calculation.
		$= \dfrac{1 \cdot 50 \times 10^{11}}{0 \cdot 8 \times 3 \times 10^{8}}$			
		$= 625\,\text{s}$	(1)		
	b)	$t' = \dfrac{t}{\sqrt{1 - \left(\dfrac{v}{c}\right)^2}}$	(1)	3	Tip: Take care not to make errors with the combination of the square and square root terms. Equation needs to be set out accurately.
		$= \dfrac{t}{0 \cdot 6}$	(1)		
		$t = 0 \cdot 6 \times 625 = 375\,\text{s}$	(1)		
				(5)	

Question		Expected response	Max. mark	Commentary with hints and tips
6	a)	$z = \dfrac{v}{c}$ (1) $= \dfrac{7{\cdot}25 \times 10^6}{3 \times 10^8}$ $= 2{\cdot}42 \times 10^{-2}$ (1)	2	You are given v and know c. This leads to selection of equation for z.
	b)	$z = \dfrac{\lambda_{observed} - \lambda_{rest}}{\lambda_{rest}}$ (1) $\lambda_{observed} = z \times \lambda_{rest} + \lambda_{rest}$ (1) $= 2{\cdot}42 \times 10^{-2} \times 656 \times 10^{-9}$ $\quad + 656 \times 10^{-9}$ (1) $= 672\,\text{nm}$ (1)	4	Rearrangement of formulae and equating to redshift can cause mistakes. Use the appropriate number of significant figures in your final answers. This means that the final answer can have no more significant figures than the value with the least number of significant figures used in the calculation. In this case, retain 3 s.f.
	c)	$v = H_0 d$ $7{\cdot}25 \times 10^6 = 2{\cdot}3 \times 10^{-18} \times d$ (1) $d = \dfrac{7{\cdot}25 \times 10^6}{2{\cdot}3 \times 10^{-18}} = 3{\cdot}15 \times 10^{24}\,\text{m}$ (1) $1\,\text{ly} = 3 \times 10^8 \times 60 \times 60 \times 24 \times 365{\cdot}25$ $\quad = 9{\cdot}467 \times 10^{15}\,\text{m}$ (1) $d = \dfrac{3{\cdot}15 \times 10^{24}}{9{\cdot}467 \times 10^{15}} = 3{\cdot}3 \times 10^8\,\text{ly}$ (1)	4	Use of Hubble equation gives answer in m. Conversion to ly is simple but easily leads to errors. One year was chosen as 365·25 days.
			(10)	
7	a)	$E = QV$ (1) $= 1{\cdot}60 \times 10^{-19} \times 22\,500$ (1) $= 3{\cdot}6 \times 10^{-15}\,\text{J}$ $3 \times E = 1{\cdot}08 \times 10^{-14}\,\text{J}$ (1)	3	Calculate energy gained using $Q \times V$ but repeat three times as proton is accelerated across the gap each time.
	b)	The protons are accelerated from P to Q **and** from Q to P. (1) This means the supply must alternate in order to accelerate the protons across the gap in both directions. (1)	2	Proton is accelerated **only** when crossing gap.
	c)	Strong magnetic fields deflect the protons (1) so that they turn and travel in the opposite direction. (1)	2	Magnetic fields *deflect* the protons. They do **not** accelerate them.
			(7)	

Question			Expected response	Max. mark	Commentary with hints and tips
8			**Sample answer** Possible responses could include some of the following concepts/points: ▶ Any life form must inhabit a planet near to a star. Distances to stars are measured in light years therefore the time to travel to Earth is measured in thousands of years. No species can survive space travel for that length of time due to oxygen, food and energy requirements. ▶ It's possible we cannot be detected. We have only emitted radio signals in the last 80 years or so and those initial signals were very weak. They would have to be detected, analysed and decoded. ▶ Life form would have to be at a suitable technological level to detect the radio signal. ▶ It is unlikely that this village in Scotland has been visited more times than anywhere else on the whole planet.	3	This is an open-ended question: a variety of physics statements and descriptions can be used to answer this question. Marks are awarded on the basis of whether the answer overall demonstrates 'no' (0 marks), 'limited' (1 mark), 'reasonable' (2 marks) or 'good' (3 marks) understanding. This type of answer might include a statement of the principles involved, a relationship or an equation, and the application of these to respond to the problem. 3 marks would be awarded to an answer which demonstrates a good understanding of the physics involved. The answer would show a good comprehension of the physics of the situation, provided in a logically correct sequence.
				(3)	
9	a)		$10^{38} \div 10^{13}$ gives 10^{25} The relative strength of the weak nuclear force is 10^{25}.	1	Order of magnitude is calculated using subtraction of indices.
	b)		W- and Z-bosons	1	Recall of the force-mediating particles.
	c)	(i)	Two up, one down (1) Two up and one down have a combined charge of +1, which is that of a proton. (1)	4	Recall and explain how quarks combine. Explain how the 'charge' of combined quarks must add up to 0 or 1.
		(ii)	Two down, one up (1) Two down and one up have a combined charge of zero, which is that of a neutron. (1)		
				(6)	

Question		Expected response	Max. mark	Commentary with hints and tips
10	a)	Uranium-235 92 protons: $92 \times 1.67262 \times 10^{-27}$ $= 153.88104 \times 10^{-27}\,kg$ (1) 143 neutrons: $143 \times 1.67429 \times 10^{-27}$ $= 239.42347 \times 10^{-27}\,kg$ (1) Total mass of constituents $= 393.30451 \times 10^{-27}\,kg$ (1) Mass of U-235: $390.206 \times 10^{-27}\,kg$ Difference in mass $= 393.30451 \times 10^{-27} - 390.206 \times 10^{-27}$ $= 3.09851 \times 10^{-27}$ $E = mc^2 = 3.09851 \times 10^{-27} \times (3 \times 10^8)^2$ $= 2.788659 \times 10^{-10}\,J$ (1) Binding energy per nucleon $= \dfrac{2.788659 \times 10^{-10}}{235}$ (1) $= 1.18666 \times 10^{-12}$ $= 1.187 \times 10^{-12}\,J$ (1)	6	It is necessary to calculate the difference between the total mass of the individual nucleons (protons and neutrons) and the actual mass of a ^{235}U nucleus. This mass defect is accounted for by the binding energy which holds the nucleons together (using $E = mc^2$ to convert mass to energy). The binding energy per nucleon is this number divided by the total number of nucleons.
	b)	A greater release of binding energy per nucleon (1) makes it more efficient for that nucleus to undergo fission rather than a fusion reaction. (1)	2	Interpretation of binding energy per nucleon. This is the key as to why fusion occurs with smaller atoms and fission with larger.
			(8)	
11	a)	$16 \times 0.15^2 = 0.36$ $4.0 \times 0.30^2 = 0.36$ $1.4 \times 0.50^2 = 0.35$ $0.64 \times 0.75^2 = 0.36$ $I \times d^2 =$ a constant value	3	This is a data-handling exercise. You must show working and how data was used to determine the relationship.
	b)	To reduce the effect of any other light being detected or measured by the meter.	1	
	c)	This will have no effect on the relationship. (1) The value of the readings on the meter may be reduced due to the filter but the relationship between irradiance and the distance should not change. (1)	2	The value of the intensity may drop but the variation with distance will obey the relationship.
			(6)	

Question		Expected response		Max. mark	Commentary with hints and tips
12	a)	$V = f \times \lambda$ $\lambda = \dfrac{v}{f} = \dfrac{3 \cdot 00 \times 10^8}{1 \cdot 25 \times 10^{15}}$ $= 2 \cdot 40 \times 10^{-7}\,\text{m}$	(1) (1)	2	You have been given frequency and velocity of light. You need to select the appropriate relationship and rearrange it.
	b)	Energy of UV radiation $E = h \times f = 6 \cdot 63 \times 10^{-34} \times 1 \cdot 25 \times 10^{15}$ $= 8 \cdot 288 \times 10^{-19}\,\text{J}$ Energy available $= 8 \cdot 288 \times 10^{-19}$ $- 7 \cdot 95 \times 10^{-19}$ $= 3 \cdot 375 \times 10^{-20}\,\text{J}$ $E_k = \dfrac{1}{2} \times m \times v^2 = 3 \cdot 375 \times 10^{-20}$ $= 0 \cdot 5 \times 9 \cdot 11 \times 10^{-31} \times v^2$ $v^2 = 2 \times \dfrac{3 \cdot 375 \times 10^{-20}}{9 \cdot 11 \times 10^{-31}}$ $v = 2 \cdot 72 \times 10^5\,\text{m s}^{-1}$	(1) (1) (1) (1) (1)	5	Use the principle of conservation of energy. Initial energy of photon will eject electron and surplus energy is transferred to electron. This energy is equated to kinetic energy and therefore velocity.
	c)	There would be an increase in the number of electrons emitted as there would be more photons striking the surface. There would be no change in the maximum velocity as the frequency of the UV has not changed.	(1) (1)	2	The increase in intensity leads to increase in number of photons only.
				(9)	
13		$T = 2 \times \pi \times \sqrt{\dfrac{L}{g}}$ $2 \cdot 15 = 2 \times \pi \times \sqrt{\dfrac{1 \cdot 15}{g}}$ Rearranging the equation gives $g = 4 \times \pi^2 \times \dfrac{L}{T^2}$ $= 4 \times 9 \cdot 87 \times \dfrac{1 \cdot 15}{4 \cdot 6225}$ $= 9 \cdot 82\,\text{m s}^{-2}$		1	In this question you are expected to perform a simple insertion of values and rearrangement of an unfamiliar relationship.

Question		Expected response	Max. mark	Commentary with hints and tips
14		**Sample answer** Possible responses could include some of the following concepts/points: ▶ Knowledge of the term efficiency: efficiency relates to energy being used for a certain purpose and is the ratio of (useful) energy output/energy input. ▶ Rating of electrical domestic appliance is r.m.s. current and/or voltage of operation. ▶ Power rating is given by $P = VI$ (each value is r.m.s.). ▶ Non-useful energy output for any device is most likely in the form of heat. Minimal amounts may be associated with light or sound. ▶ It is unlikely therefore that a heater can 'waste' energy because the heat transfer is the intended output purpose of the device. As a result this heater cannot be any more efficient.	3	This is an open-ended question: a variety of physics statements and descriptions can be used to answer this question. Marks are awarded on the basis of whether the answer overall demonstrates 'no' (0 marks), 'limited' (1 mark), 'reasonable' (2 marks) or 'good' (3 marks) understanding. This type of answer might include a statement of the principles involved, a relationship or an equation, and the application of these to respond to the problem. Three marks would be awarded to an answer which demonstrates a good understanding of the physics involved. The answer would show a good comprehension of the physics of the situation, provided in a logically correct sequence.
			(3)	
15	a)	$n_1 \sin\theta_1 = n_2 \sin\theta_2$ (1) $1{\cdot}55 \times \sin 22 = 1 \sin\theta_2 = 0{\cdot}58$ (1) $\theta_2 = 35{\cdot}5 = 36°$ (1)	3	The problem here is that the triangle is air within the glass block. Care has to be taken to ensure the appropriate refractive index is used at the correct position. n_1 is 1·55, n_2 is 1.
	b)	 Ray strikes glass at other side of triangle at an angle of 24° to the normal.	3	1 mark for identifying the top triangle. 1 mark for calculating the angles of triangle. 1 mark for subtracting from 90 to angle of incidence.
			(6)	

Question			Expected response	Max. mark	Commentary with hints and tips
16	a)	(i)	$\dfrac{1}{R_T} = \dfrac{1}{R_1} + \dfrac{1}{R_2}$ (1) $= \dfrac{1}{30} + \dfrac{1}{20} = \dfrac{5}{60} = \dfrac{1}{12}$ $R_T = 12\,\Omega$ Total $R = 12\,\Omega + 1\cdot5\,\Omega = 13\cdot5\,\Omega$ (1) $I = \dfrac{\text{e.m.f.}}{\text{total } R}$ $= \dfrac{12\cdot0}{13\cdot5} = 0\cdot889\,\text{A}$ (1)	3	Calculate the combined resistance of the resistors then add to the internal resistance of the cell for total resistance.
		(ii)	V from supply $= I \times R$ (1) $= 0\cdot889 \times 12 = 10\cdot668 = 10\cdot7\,\text{V}$ (1)	2	Determine the current drawn from the cell then use this value the voltage across the external resistors.
	b)		The resistor should be placed in series with the supply but not as part of the parallel circuit. (1) This would increase the total resistance, which would reduce the current and therefore increase the voltage from the supply. (1)	2	The first mark is for the correct placement and the second mark is for the correct explanation.
				(7)	
17	a)		$I_1 = \dfrac{V}{R_1} = \dfrac{12}{30} = 0\cdot4\,\text{A}$ (1) $I_2 = \dfrac{V}{R_2} = \dfrac{12}{15} = 0\cdot8\,\text{A}$ (1) Total current $= 1\cdot2\,\text{A}$ (1)	3	Treat each branch in the same way you would a parallel circuit problem. The uncharged capacitors have no bearing on the initial charging current.
	b)		$Q = CV$ (1) $= 160 \times 10^{-6} \times 12 = 0\cdot0192\,\text{C}$ (1) $Q \times 2 = 0\cdot003\,84 = 3\cdot8 \times 10^{-3}\,\text{C}$ (1)	3	Each capacitor will charge to the same potential and therefore the same amount of charge will be transferred. Calculate charge for one then multiply by 2.
	c)		1 mark for graphs having the correct downward sloping shape. 1 mark for a comparative shape similar to those shown.	2	The charging current in capacitor 1 is lower due to the higher value resistor connected in series with it. Capacitor 2 has a higher initial charging current but a smaller charging time as both capacitors have the same value. The same amount of charge will transfer to them.

Question			Expected response		Max. mark	Commentary with hints and tips
d)	**(i)**		$R_T = 64 + 30 = 94\,\Omega$	(1)	3	The key point here is to treat the circuit as a series circuit with two resistors, $30\,\Omega$ and $64\,\Omega$.
			$I = \dfrac{V}{R_T}$			
			$= \dfrac{12}{94}$	(1)		
			$= 0 \cdot 127$			
			$= 0 \cdot 13\,\text{A}$	(1)		
	(ii)		Current from capacitor 2:		4	The key point here is to treat the circuit as a series circuit with two resistors, $15\,\Omega$ and $64\,\Omega$.
			$R_T = 64 + 15 = 79\,\Omega$	(1)		It would be easy but wrong to take the $15\,\Omega$ and $30\,\Omega$ resistors and treat them as a parallel circuit. The circuits have to be treated separately. This is a type of circuit where we combine two sources, not commonly seen.
			$I = \dfrac{V}{R_T}$			
			$= \dfrac{12}{79}$	(1)		
			$= 0 \cdot 152$			
			$= 0 \cdot 15\,\text{A}$	(1)		
			Combined current:			
			$0 \cdot 127\,\text{A} + 0 \cdot 152\,\text{A} = 0 \cdot 28\,\text{A}$	(1)		
					(15)	
					[130]	